ECHOES

ECHOES

compiled by

LIONEL JACKSON
Lecturer in English, Moray House College of Education

LONDON
G. BELL & SONS LTD
1971

ISBN 0 7135 1614 3

Printed in Great Britain by
Butler & Tanner Ltd,
Frome and London

Preface

A television play, a pop-song or an argument may amuse, excite or disturb you. A good poem can also set up reverberations of thought and feeling. It may, as Norman MacCaig recently said, 'brush the nerve-ends'. It can create echoes – which may return.

I hope you will find the poems collected here to be of this type. Some of them will perhaps fix your attention straight away with a picture, person, incident or rhythm. But most do not stop there – they make a sly assault. Some have surprising or complex things to say about life and about you, and you may need to come back to them several times to get the message in full.

I have grouped the poems into six broad themes: between them they show man coming to terms with himself, his fellow-creatures and his world. The groups should provide some interesting contrasts and comparisons.

In each section are some photographs which approach the theme from fresh angles. You may like to use them as starting points for talking or writing. More specific invitations for writing or discussion are given at the end of each section, on single poems or linked groups. Some poems are left without comment. For those who wish to explore the themes further I have given reading lists, though these are no more than travel guides.

It is the poems themselves, however, that matter most, and I hope you will be able to incorporate at least some of them into your own 'personal anthology'.

Contents

I Kith and Kin

III *Earth, Air, Fire and Water*

IV *Other Kingdom*

V New Men

VI Dreams and Visions

Acknowledgments

Thanks are here expressed for permission to include copyright poems to the following or their executors and to the publishers of their work:

Conrad Aiken: 'Nuit blanche: North end' from *Collected Poems* (Oxford University Press), copyright 1942 by Conrad Aiken   George Barker: 'On a friend's escape from drowning', 'To my mother' from *Collected Poems 1930–1955* (Faber & Faber)   Bruce Beaver: 'Cow dance' (*The Bulletin*, Sydney), by permission of Bruce Beaver   John Betjeman: 'Five o'clock shadow', Meditation on the A30', 'Inexpensive progress' from *High and Low* (Murray)   Elizabeth Bishop: 'The fish' from *Selected Poems* (Chatto & Windus)   Thomas Blackburn: 'A smell of burning' from *A Smell of Burning* (Putnam)   John Blight: 'Death of a whale' from *A Beachcomber's Diary* (*The Bulletin*, Sydney), by permission of John Blight   Edmund Blunden: 'An international football match', 'The scientists' from *Poems 1930–1940* (Collins), by permission of A. D. Peters & Co.   Gordon Bottomley: 'To iron-founders and others', by permission of C. C. Abbott   Robert Bridges: 'London snow' from *The Poetical Works of Robert Bridges* (Clarendon Press)   Charles Causley: 'Balland of the bread man' from *Underneath the Water* (Macmillan)   John Clare: 'Song: I peeled . . .' from *The Later Poems of John Clare* (Manchester University Press)   Alex Comfort: 'The charmer' (Eyre & Spottiswoode)   e. e. cummings: 'little tree', 'here's a little mouse' from *Complete Poems 1913–1935* (MacGibbon & Kee).

Robert Davies: 'Leather jackets, bikes and birds' from *Every Man Will Shout*, ed. Mansfield and Armstrong (Clarendon Press)   W. H. Davies: 'The hermit', 'The heap of rags' from *The Complete Poems of W. H. Davies* (Cape), with acknowledgment to Mrs H. M. Davies   Walter de la Mare: 'Drugged', the Literary Trustees of Walter de la Mare represented by the Society of Authors   T. S. Eliot: Extract from *The Family Reunion* in *Collected Plays of Robert Frost* (Cape and Holt, Rinehart & Winston)   Roy Fuller: 'Autobiography of a lungworm' from *Collected Poems* (Deutsch)   Thom Gunn: 'Taylor Street' from *Touch* (Faber & Faber), 'On the move', 'Elvis Presley' from *The Sense of Movement* (Faber & Faber)   Thomas Hardy: 'The convergence of the twain' from *The Collected Poems of Thomas Hardy* (Macmillan), with permission of the Trustees of the Hardy Estate   Anthony Hecht: 'Lizards and snakes' from *The Hard Hours* (Oxford University Press)   A. L. Hendriks: 'An old Jamaican woman thinks . . .', 'Christmas' from *On this Mountain* (Deutsch)   David Holbrook: 'Unholy marriage' from *Imaginings* (Putnam), by permission of David Holbrook   Ted Hughes: 'Her husband', 'The rescue', 'Ghost crabs' from *Wodwo* (Faber & Faber); 'The jaguar' from *The Hawk in the Rain* (Faber & Faber).

D. H. Lawrence: 'Baby running barefoot', 'Man and bat' from *The Complete Poems of D. H. Lawrence* (Heinemann), with acknowledgment to Lawrence Polinger Ltd and the Estate of the late Mrs Frieda Lawrence   C. Day Lewis: 'Flight to Italy' from *Collected Poems 1954* (Cape and the Hogarth Press)   F. L. Lucas: 'Beleaguered cities' from *Time and Memory* (Hogarth Press) with permission of Mrs Elna Lucas   Edward Lucie-Smith: 'The lesson' from *A Tropical Childhood and Other Poems* (Oxford University Press) Norman MacCaig: 'True ways of knowing', 'Traffic stop', 'Struck by lightning' from *Measures* (Chatto & Windus); 'Basking Shark' (*The Scotsman*), by permission of Norman MacCaig   Louis MacNeice: 'Birmingham' from *Collected Poems* (Faber & Faber)   Harold Massingham: 'Puritan of the pits' from *Black Bull Guarding Apples* (Longmans Green)   Edgar Lee Masters: 'Butch Weldy' from *Spoon River Anthology* (Werner Laurie)   Ray Mathew: 'Our father', 'Love and marriage' from *South of the Equator* (Angus & Robertson), by permission of Ray Mathew   Edwin Muir: 'The interrogation', 'The labyrinth' from *Collected Poems 1921–1958* (Faber & Faber)   Ogden Nash: 'It's about time' from *Private Dining Room*; 'What almost every woman knows . . .' from *Family Reunion* (Dent)   Norman Nicholson: 'Millom Old Quarry', 'Cleator Moor' from *Selected Poems* (Faber & Faber)   Leslie Norris: 'The quarrel', 'Dead boys', 'October sun' from *Finding Gold* (Chatto & Windus).

Philip Oakes: 'After the wedding' from *In the Affirmative* (Deutsch)   William Plomer: 'In the snake park' from *Collected Poems* (Cape)   Alexander Reid: 'Dog' from *Steps to a Viewpoint* (Dakers), by permission of Alexander Reid   Alan Ross: 'Bus boycott' from *African Negatives* (Eyre & Spottiswoode)   Carl Sandburg: 'Psalm of those who go forth before daybreak' from *Cornhuskers* (Cape and Holt, Rinehart & Winston)   Vernon Scannell: 'My father's face', 'A day on the river' from *A Sense of Danger* (Putnam), 'Walking wounded' from *Walking Wounded* (Eyre & Spottiswoode), by permission of Vernon Scannell   Edith Sitwell: 'Still falls the rain' from *Collected Poems* (Macmillan)   Stephen Spender: 'The pylons' from *Collected Poems* (Faber & Faber)   Dylan Thomas: 'A refusal to mourn', 'Fern Hill' from *Collected Poems* (Dent), with acknowledgment to the Trustees for the Copyrights of the late Dylan Thomas   R. S. Thomas: 'The Welsh hill country', 'Cynddylan on a tractor' from *Song at the Year's Turning* (Hart-Davis)   John Updike: 'The one-year-old', 'Snapshots', 'Ex-basketball player' from *Hoping for a Hoopoe* (Gollancz)   Rex Warner: 'Nile fishermen' (Bodley Head)   Vernon Watkins: 'The heron', 'Ballad of the trial of Sodom' from *The Death Bell* (Faber & Faber)   Judith Wright: 'Woman to man' from *The Moving Image* (Meanjin Press, Melbourne)   W. B. Yeats: 'An Irish airman foresees his death' from *Collected Poems* (Macmillan), with permission of M. B. Yeats.

Thanks are due to the copyright owners as following for permission to reproduce photographs on the pages mentioned:

The Times, pp. 4, 34, 64, 108   Eric Johnson, p. 10   Thomas A. Wilkie, pp. 18, 68, 74, 78, 84   Keystone, pp. 24, 44, 94, 104   Sport and General, pp. 38, 50   Zoological Society of London, p. 98   Associated Press, p. 122   Rolls-Royce Ltd, p. 128   Fox Photos, pp. 134, 138   London-Express, p. 150   C. J. Williamson, p. 154   Feature-Pix, p. 162   Dennis Shepherd, p. 166   Dennis Coutts, p. 170.

I Kith and Kin

(After reading the appropriate chapter in *Infant and Child
in the Culture of Today,* by Arnold Gesell and Frances Ilg)

Wakes wet; is promptly toileted;
Jargons to himself; is fed;

Executively grips a cup;
Quadrupedal, will sit up

Unaided; laughs; applauds; enjoys
Baths and manipulative toys;

Socialises (parents: shun
Excess acculturation);

Demonstrates prehension; will
Masticate yet seldom spill;

Creeps (gross motor drives are strong);
And jargons, jargons all day long.

**The
One-Year-Old**

*John Updike
b. 1932*

*

When the white feet of the baby beat across the grass
The little white feet nod like white flowers in a wind,
They poise and run like puffs of wind that pass
Over water where the weeds are thinned.

And the sight of their white playing in the grass
Is winsome as a robin's song, so fluttering;
Or like two butterflies that settle on a glass
Cup for a moment, soft little wing-beats uttering.

**Baby
Running
Barefoot**

*D. H. Lawrence
1885–1930*

1

And I wish that the baby would tack across here to me
Like a wind-shadow running on a pond, so she could stand
With two little bare white feet upon my knee
And I could feel her feet in either hand

Cool as syringa buds in morning hours,
Or firm and silken as young peony flowers.

We Are Seven

William
Wordsworth
1770–1850

– A simple Child,
That lightly draws its breath,
And feels its life in every limb,
What should it know of death?

I met a little cottage Girl:
She was eight years old, she said;
Her hair was thick with many a curl
That clustered round her head.

She had a rustic, woodland air,
And she was wildly clad:
Her eyes were fair, and very fair;
– Her beauty made me glad.

'Sisters and brothers, little maid,
How many may you be?'
'How many? Seven in all,' she said,
And wondering looked at me.

'And where are they? I pray you tell.'
She answered, 'Seven are we;
And two of us at Conway dwell,
And two are gone to sea.

'Two of us in the church-yard lie,
My sister and my brother;
And, in the church-yard cottage, I
Dwell near them with my mother.'

'You say that two at Conway dwell,
And two are gone to sea,
Yet ye are seven! I pray you tell,
Sweet Maid, how this may be.'

Then did the little Maid reply,
'Seven boys and girls are we;
Two of us in the church-yard lie,
Beneath the church-yard tree.'

'You run about, my little Maid,
Your limbs they are alive;
If two are in the church-yard laid,
Then ye are only five.'

'Their graves are green, they may be seen,'
The little Maid replied,
'Twelve steps or more from my mother's door,
And they are side by side.

'My stockings there I often knit,
My kerchief there I hem;
And there upon the ground I sit,
And sing a song to them.

'And often after sun-set, Sir,
When it is light and fair,
I take my little porringer,
And eat my supper there.

'The first that died was sister Jane;
In bed she moaning lay,
Till God released her of her pain;
And then she went away.

'So in the church-yard she was laid;
And, when the grass was dry,
Together round her grave we played,
My brother John and I.

'And when the ground was white with snow,
And I could run and slide,
My brother John was forced to go,
And he lies by her side.'

'How many are you, then,' said I,
'If they two are in heaven?'
Quick was the little Maid's reply,
'O Master! we are seven.'

'But they are dead; those two are dead!
Their spirits are in heaven!'
'Twas throwing words away; for still
The little Maid would have her will,
And said, 'Nay, we are seven!'

*

She said my father had whiskers and looked like God;
that he swore like a fettler, drank like a bottle;
used to run away from mother, left money for food;
called us by numbers; had a belt with a buckle.

On Sunday was churchday. We children walked behind.
He'd wear a stiff collar. He'd say good-morning.
And we made jokes about him, we were afraid
because already we understood about hating.

When we'd left the church that was so nice and still,
the minister would let us give the bells a telling –
four dong-dells; and we'd decide that Nell's
was to be the end of the world; it was time for going.

When we got home he'd take off his collar, and his shoes;
and his Sunday-special braces; and we'd whisper,
he's not like God. So that he'd belt us for the noise,
and we'd yell. And on Mondays he'd run away from mother.

*Our
Father*

*Ray Mathew
b. 1929*

Iippies

A Smell of Burning

Thomas Blackburn
b. 1916

After each savage, hysterical episode,
So common with us, my mother would sniff the air
And murmur, 'Nurse, would you look at the upstairs fire,
I smell burning, something's alight somewhere.'
But a red coal never was found, or jet of gas,
Scorching dry board, or paint-work beginning to melt;
And too young was I in that nursery time to guess
What smoking, subjective fire she really smelt.
Nowadays I know quite well from hers they came,
And my father's mouth, when the hot tongues crackled and spat;
But what mattered then was a trick of dodging flame,
And keeping some breath alive in the heat of it.
I have it still that inbred dodging trick;
But always – when the fire beset – I see them turning,
My parents, to name elsewhere their sour fire reak,
And touch myself and know what's really burning.

From The Family Reunion

Part II,
Scene 1

T. S. Eliot
1888–1965

HARRY: What about my mother?
Everything has always been referred back to mother.
When we were children, before we went to school,
The rule of conduct was simply pleasing mother;
Misconduct was simply being unkind to mother;
What was wrong was whatever made her suffer,
And whatever made her happy was what was virtuous –
Though never very happy, I remember. That was why
We all felt like failures, before we had begun.
When we came back, for the school holidays,
They were not holidays, but simply a time
In which we were supposed to make up to mother
For all the weeks during which she had not seen us
Except at half term, and seeing us then
Only seemed to make her more unhappy, and made us
Feel more guilty, and so we misbehaved
Next day at school, in order to be punished,
For punishment made us feel less guilty. Mother
Never punished us, but made us feel guilty.
I think that the things that are taken for granted
At home, make a deeper impression upon the children
Than what they are told.

Most near, most dear, most loved and most far,
Under the window where I often found her
Sitting as huge as Asia, seismic with laughter,
Gin and chicken helpless in her Irish hand,
Irresistible as Rabelais, but most tender for
The lame dogs and hurt birds that surround her, –
She is a procession no one can follow after
But be like a little dog following a brass band.

She will not glance up at the bomber, or condescend
To drop her gin and scuttle to a cellar,
But lean on the mahogany table like a mountain
Whom only faith can move, and so I send
O all my faith and all my love to tell her
That she will move from mourning into morning.

*George Barker
b. 1913*

Booming sirens were the colliers' church bells,
Black sweat and strenuous torso their fellowship.
In tunnels timber-propt below street-level, jaws
Mashing black plug to spittle, pitted blokes hacked seams
In choke-stythe druggier than the gas of poppies,
The chesty, dead smell of coal, sensation of catarrh.

This their religion: Sundays were saved
For Cleethorpes, collar-studs, snoring off local ale
Or training whippets in what remained of England;
For day-long docility with sullen wives
Or electric rage earthing through stools and vases;
For even effeminacy at first primroses.

If eyes in grimy masks were not diamonds,
They were dulled from mines of grief at pit-perishings,
When a big owl boomed and summoned their stunned
Princesses who'd pricked their fingers on pit-head
Spindle wheels, now penny-wise, stoic in glooms of shawls,
Resigned to the tender sponging of men's bodies,

*Puritan
of the
Pits*

*Harold
Massingham
b. 1932*

7

As if they were dusting inestimable china: then,
Back to their purses, frying-pans and bakery –
Their pit men, quietly oathing systems away,
Back to their tunnels, tap-rooms, Sundays,
Toil and contented toping, pay-day dominoeing,
Supperless belching to bed, wives bristling with strike.

My father, except he scanted alcohol
To two or three cosy, Christmas sherries,
Indulgently as swear-words among his mates,
Was one of them. He half-mastered, like hundreds more,
A scruffy house, a cockroach-nest, its design
A tenth-rate, cash-making impudence. His life's

Included clogs, the brothers Wesley, nineteen-
Twenty-six, cold bottled tea. I've heard him slander
Incomprehensible, fancy Churches,
Because old rope pit-ponies used to tug coal-loads,
Not silk and satin threads: delicatessen too,
O fragrant tit-bits, he flung to poodles,

With that taut, seventeenth-century damnation face.
Prodigal dropper of aitches, his vowels so broad
They were cosmic, my puritan of the pits,
For fifty years too penniless for Switzerland
But laboured in coal-smoke, what can I say
For his retiring days? I know that in his blood's

Canal move recollections like lethargic barges –
Fathering a solitary lad; the children's
Twittering Whitsuntides now dulled to wood-dove coos;
Watching his wife wane or make a rare wintry willow,
Something that cost him eleven sexless years; –
Or maybe clogs and a lorry's landslide of coal

Startle some old sparrows, there in the street
Narrow as a chapel-aisle. A certain childishness,
Deafness, grey hair and carboned lungs are this man now,
Veins like old rope. I visit him too rarely,
Do not know what to say in letters. But once back
Embarrassingly in smoky Mexborough, my romancing eyes

8

Found a few elders, my father one of them,
Heart-wits down to Davy-flame – though brighter
By Dolly Daydream, grandchildren, spilt beer;
And what with aitches house-top hoisted, and somehow
Seamless meetings of mates, I knew I had glimpsed
The passing of primroses, whippets and rich pennies,

Of generations of poverties now too old
To taste prosperity, or call it other than
An air-conditioned glittering kitchen of tin-cans:
I knew I had glimpsed the very ghosting of smoke,
Like seeing, as once with a casual car-window glance,
The specific, peculiar silence of a disused mine.

Each morning, when I shave, I see his face,
Or something like a sketch of it gone wrong;
The artist caught, it seems, more than a trace
Of that uneasy boldness and the strong
Fear behind the stare which tried to shout
How tough its owner was, inviting doubt.

And though this face is altogether more
Loosely put together, and indeed
A lot less handsome, weaker in the jaw
And softer in the mouth, I feel no need
To have it reassembled, made a better
Copy of the face of its begetter.

I do not mind because my mouth is not
That lipless hyphen, military, stern;
He had the face that faces blade and shot
In schoolboys' tales, and even schoolboys learn
To laugh at it. But they've not heard it speak
Those bayonet words that guard the cruel and the weak.

For weakness was his one consistency;
And when I scrape the soapy fluff away
I see that he bequeathed this gift to me
Along with various debts I cannot pay.
But he gave, too, this mirror-misting breath
Whose mercy dims the looking-glass of death;

*My
Father's
Face*

*Vernon
Scannell
b. 1922*

Young cricketers

For which kind accident I thank him now
And, though I cannot love him, feel a sort
Of salty tenderness, remembering how,
The prude and lecher in him moiled and fought
Their roughhouse in the dark ring of his pride
And killed each other when his body died.

This morning, as I shave, I find I can
Forgive the blows, the meanness and the lust,
The ricocheting arsenal of a man
Who groaned groin-deep in hope's ironic dust;
But those eyes in the glass regard the living
Features with distaste, quite unforgiving.

It was late last Saturday evening
I went to see my dear,
The candles were all burning
And the moon shone bright and clear.
I rapped on her window
To ease her of her pain,
She rose and let me in
And then barred the door again.

I like well your behaviour
And this I often say –
I cannot rest contented
While you are far away.
But the roads they were so muddy
I cannot roam about,
So roll me in your arms, love,
And blow the candle out.

Your father and your mother
In yonder room do lie,
A-huggin' one another,
So why not you and I?
A-huggin' one another,
Without a fear or doubt
So roll me in your arms, love,
And blow the candle out.

Blow
the
Candle
Out

Anonymous

11

And if we prove successful, love,
Please name it after me,
Hug it neat and kiss it sweet
And dap it on your knee.
When my three years are ended
And my time it is run out,
Then I will prove my indebtedness
By blowing the candle out.

Arab Love Song

Francis
Thompson
1859–1907

The hunched camels of the night*
Trouble the bright
And silver waters of the moon.
The maiden of the morn will soon
Through Heaven stray and sing,
Star gathering.

Now while the dark about our loves is strewn,
Light of my dark, blood of my heart, O come!
And night will catch her breath up, and be dumb.

Leave thy father, leave thy mother
And thy brother;
Leave the black tents of thy tribe apart!
Am I not thy father and thy brother,
And thy mother?
And thou – what needest with thy tribe's black tents
Who hast the red pavilion of my heart?

* Cloud shapes
observed by
travellers in
the East

Frankie and Johnny

Anonymous

Frankie and Johnny were lovers, O, how that couple could love.
Swore to be true to each other, true as the stars above.
He was her man, but he done her wrong.

Frankie she was his woman, everybody knows.
She spent one hundred dollars for a suit of Johnny's clothes.
He was her man, but he done her wrong.

Frankie and Johnny went walking, Johnny in his bran' new suit,
'O good Lawd,' says Frankie, 'but don't my Johnny look cute?'
He was her man, but he done her wrong.

Frankie went down to Memphis; she went on the evening train.
She paid one hundred dollars for Johnny a watch and chain.
He was her man, but he done her wrong.

Frankie went down to the corner, to buy a glass of beer;
She says to the fat bartender, 'Has my lovin' man bin here?
He was my man, but he done me wrong.'

'Ain't gonna tell you no story, ain't gonna tell you no lie,
I seen your man 'bout an hour ago with a girl named Alice Fry.
If he's your man, he doin' you wrong.'

Frankie went back to the hotel, she didn't go there for fun,
Under her long red kimono she toted a forty-four gun.
He was her man, but he done her wrong.

Frankie went down to the hotel, looked in the window so high,
There was her lovin' Johnny a-lovin' up Alice Fry;
He was her man, but he done her wrong.

Frankie threw back her kimono; took out the old forty-four;
Roota-toot-toot, three times she shot, right through that hotel door.
She shot her man, 'cause he done her wrong.

Johnny grabbed off his Stetson. 'O good Lord, Frankie, don't shoot.'
But Frankie put her finger on the trigger, and the gun went roota-
        toot-toot.
He was her man, but she shot him down.

'Roll me over easy, roll me over slow,
Roll me over easy, boys, 'cause my wounds are hurting me so,
I was her man, but I done her wrong.'

With the first shot Johnny staggered; with the second shot he fell;
When the third bullet hit him, there was a new man's face in hell.
He was her man, but he done her wrong.

Frankie heard a rumblin' away down underground.
Maybe it was Johnny where she had shot him down.
He was her man, and she done him wrong.

'Oh bring on your rubber-tired hearses, bring on your rubber-tired
    hacks,
They're takin' my Johnny to the buryin' ground but they'll never bring
    him back.
He was my man, but he done me wrong.'

The judge said to the jury, 'It's as plain as plain can be.
This woman shot her man, so it's murder in the second degree.
He was her man, though he done her wrong.'

Now it wasn't murder in the second degree, it wasn't murder in the
    third.
Frankie simply dropped her man, like a hunter drops a bird.
He was her man, but he done her wrong.

'Oh, put me in that dungeon. Oh, put me in that cell.
Put me where the northeast wind blows from the southeast corner
    of hell.
I shot my man 'cause he done me wrong.'

Frankie walked up to the scaffold, as calm as a girl could be,
She turned her eyes to heaven and said, 'Good Lord, I'm coming to
    thee.
He was my man, and I done him wrong.'

The Furious Gun

*Sir Thomas
Wyatt
c. 1503–42*

The furious gun in his most raging ire,
When that the bowl is rammed in too sore,
And that the flame cannot part from the fire,
Cracks in sunder, and in the air do roar
The shivered pieces. So doth my desire,
Whose flame increaseth aye from more to more;
Which to let out, I dare not look, nor speak;
So inward force my heart doth all to break.

14

Desire that all men have is all my love.
But the girl reads magazines with glossy covers,
Denies the self-in-time that she might have,
Declares that she needs love and never lovers.

Habitual's the thing I most despise.
But the girl talks home and marriage, licensed lovers,
Denies the act, the play, the hope of prize,
Declares she needs what never love discovers.

I should have known, those loving-days ago,
The girl in her hid woman and not lover
For when we fell upon the floor to crow
She saw the carpet needed sweeping over

Though she said nothing then; I had my way.
But she it is who names the wedding day.

After the wedding, after the buckshot of rice, the jokes at the
      reception,
After viewing gifts, posing for pictures, the ride in the hired car, they
      are alone

In a strange room, the gas fire popping, the sea outside
Thrashing the sand. A mirror fondly frames them: groom and bride.

They have kept the address secret. No bawdy telegram
('Report speed and position at midnight') will find them.

They are a world away. In a big bed
They gorge themselves on love, eating each other like bread.

Now they are holy, they may never be holy again.
This is the true sacrament. Their flesh is one.

Waking at nightfall she will find him there,
Breathing her body's breath, a naked stranger

Whose beard barks her face, whose hairy legs
Knot hers like string. Their dialogues

*Love
and
Marriage*

*Ray Mathew
b. 1929*

*After
the
Wedding*

*Philip Oakes
b. 1928*

Spoken in whispers between the chime of clocks,
Cisterns flushing, and the melting of flesh like wax

Will be forgotten. They will remember first light,
The shape of a window, traffic in the street;

A few words such as love, want, now: imperatives
Like wrangler's irons branding their lives.

Nothing more, except this: a memory, keen as childhood
Of being somewhere first, a clearing in the wood,

A sea garden, greedy with anemones. No track,
No artfully dropped pebbles point the way back.

But long after the bed is empty, the room
Vacated, the honeymoon over, each will come

Back to the point of entry, willing it to exist
Sometimes improbably in a land laid waste.

Her Husband

Ted Hughes
b. 1930

Comes home dull with coal-dust deliberately
To grime the sink and foul towels and let her
Learn with scrubbing brush and scrubbing board
The stubborn character of money.

And let her learn through what kind of dust
He has earned his thirst and the right to quench it
And what sweat he has exchanged for his money
And the blood-weight of money. He'll humble her

With new light on her obligations.
The fried, woody chips, kept warm two hours in the oven,
Are only part of her answer.
Hearing the rest, he slams them to the fire back

And is away round the house-end singing
'Come back to Sorrento' in a voice
Of resounding corrugated iron.
Her back has bunched into a hump as an insult.

For they will have their rights.
Their jurors are to be assembled
From the little crumbs of soot. Their brief
Goes straight up to heaven and nothing more is heard of it.

How simple was the relationship between the sexes in the days of
  Francesca di Rimini;
Men were menacing, women were womeny.
When confronted with women, men weren't expected to understand
  them;
Their alternatives were, if accepted, to embrace, if rejected, to unhand
  them.
I attribute much of our modern tension
To a misguided striving for intersexual comprehension.
It's about time to realise, brethren, as best we can,
That a woman is not just a female man.
How bootless, then, to chafe
When they are late because they have no watch with them, all eleven of
  their watches are on the dressing table or in the safe;
How fruitless to pout
Because they believe that every time the dog scratches it really wants to
  go out;
Give your tongue to the cat
When you ask what they want for their birthday and they say, Oh any-
  thing, and you get anything, and then discover it should have been
  anything but that.
Pocket the gold, fellows, ask not why it glisters;
As Margaret Fuller accepted the universe, so let us accept her sisters.
Women would I think be easier nationalised
Than rationalised,
And the battle of the sexes can be a most enjoyable scrimmage
If you'll only stop trying to create woman in your own image.

It's
About
Time

Ogden Nash
b. 1902

Parents

Husbands are things that wives have to get used to putting up with,
And with whom they breakfast with and sup with.
They interfere with the discipline of nurseries,
And forget anniversaries,
And when they have been particularly remiss
They think they can cure everything with a great big kiss,
And when you tell them about something they have done they just look
    unbearably patient and smile a superior smile,
And think, Oh she'll get over it after a while.
And they always drink cocktails faster than they can assimilate them,
And if you look in their direction they act as if they were martyrs and
    you were trying to sacrifice, or immolate them.
And they never want to get up or go to bed at the same time as you do,
And when you perform some simple rite like putting cold cream on your
    face or applying a touch of lipstick they seem to think you are up to
    some kind of black magic like a priestess of Voodoo,
And they are brave and calm and cool and collected about the ailments
    of the person they have promised to honor and cherish,
But the minute they get a sniffle or a stomachache of their own, why
    you'd think they were about to perish,
And when you are alone with them they ignore all the minor courtesies,
    and as for airs and graces they utterly lack them,
But when there are a lot of people around they hand you so many chairs
    and ashtrays and sandwiches and butter you with such bowings and
    scrapings that you want to smack them.
Husbands are indeed an irritating form of life,
And yet through some quirk of Providence most of them are really very
    deeply esconced in the affection of their wife.

*What
Almost
Every
Woman
Knows
Sooner
or Later*

*Ogden Nash
b. 1902*

*

The eyeless labourer in the night,
the selfless, shapeless seed I hold,
builds for its resurrection day –
silent and swift and deep from sight
foresees the unimagined light.

This is no child with a child's face;
this has no name to name it by;
yet you and I have known it well.
This our hunter and our chase,
the third who lay in our embrace.

*Woman
to Man*

*Judith Wright
b. 1915*

19

This is the strength that your arm knows,
the arc of flesh that is my breast,
the precise crystals of our eyes.
This is the blood's wild tree that grows
the intricate and folded rose.

This is the maker and the made;
this is the question and reply;
the blind head butting at the dark,
the blaze of light along the blade.
Oh hold me, for I am afraid.

Snap-shots

John Updike
b. 1932

How good of Mrs Metz! The blur
Must be your cousin Christopher.

A scenic shot Jim took near Lyme.
Those rocks seemed lovely at the time.

And here's a product of the days
When Jim went through his gnarled tree phase.

The man behind the man in shorts –
His name is Shorer, Shaw, or Schwartz.

The kids at play. This must be Keith.
Can that be Wilma underneath?

I'd give my life to know why Josh
Sat next to Mrs McIntosh.

Jim looked so well in checkered clothes.
I was much slimmer than this shows.

Yes, Jim and I were so in love.
That hat: what *was* I thinking of?

This disappointed Mrs Striker.
I don't know why, it's very like her.

The dog is Skip. He loved to play.
We had to have him put away.

I guess these people are the Wrens.
There was some water on the lens.

This place is where I was inspired
To – stop me, if your eyes are tired.

Sweetest love, I do not goe,
　　For wearinesse of thee,
Nor in hope the world can show
　　A fitter Love for mee;
　　　　But since that I
Must dye at last, 'tis best,
To use my selfe in jest
　　Thus by fain'd deaths to dye;

Yesternight the Sunne went hence,
　　And yet is here to day,
He hath no desire nor sense,
　　Nor halfe so short a way:
　　　　Then feare not mee,
But beleeve that I shall make
Speedier journeyes, since I take
　　More wings and spurres then hee.

O how feeble is mans power,
　　That if good fortune fall,
Cannot adde another houre,
　　Nor a lost houre recall!
　　　　But come bad chance,
And wee joyne to'it our strength,
And we teach it art and length,
　　It selfe o'r us to'advance.

Song

John Donne
1572–1631

21

When thou sigh'st, thou sigh'st not winde,
    But sigh'st my soule away,
When thou weep'st, unkindly kinde,
    My life's blood doth decay.
        It cannot bee
That thou lov'st mee, as thou say'st,
If in thine my life thou waste,
    Thou art the best of mee.

Let not thy divining heart
    Forethinke me any ill,
Destiny may take thy part,
    And may thy feares fulfill;
        But thinke that wee
Are but turn'd aside to sleepe;
They who one another keepe
    Alive, ne'r parted bee.

True Ways of Knowing

Norman
MacCaig
b. 1911

Not an ounce excessive, not an inch too little,
Our easy reciprocations. You let me know
The way a boat would feel, if it could feel,
The intimate support of water.

The news you bring me has been news forever,
So that I understand what a stone would say
If only a stone could speak. Is it sad a grassblade
Can't know how it is lovely?

Is it sad that you can't know, except by hearsay
(My gossiping failing words) that you are the way
A water is that can clench its palm and crumple
A boat's confiding timbers?

But that's excessive, and too little. Knowing
The way a circle would describe its roundness,
We touch two selves and feel, complete and gentle,
The intimate support of being.

The way that flight would feel a bird flying
(If it could feel) is the way a space that's in
A stone that's in a water would know itself
If it had our way of knowing.

What's the world to you?
Much. I was born of woman, and drew milk,
As sweet as charity, from human breasts.
I think, articulate, I laugh and weep,
And exercise all functions of a man.
How then should I and any man that lives
Be strangers to each other? Pierce my vein,
Take of the crimson stream meandering there,
And catechise it well; apply thy glass,
Search it, and prove now if it be not blood
Congenial with thine own: and, if it be,
What edge of subtlety canst thou suppose
Keen enough, wise and skilful as thou art,
To cut the link of brotherhood, by which
One common Maker bound me to the kind?

*The Link
of
Brother-
hood*

*William
Cowper
(from 'The
Task', Bk. III)
1731–1800*

*

Mary stood in the kitchen
Baking a loaf of bread.
An angel flew in through the window.
We've a job for you, he said.

God in his big gold heaven,
Sitting in his big blue chair,
Wanted a mother for his little son.
Suddenly saw you there.

Mary shook and trembled,
It isn't true what you say.
Don't say that, said the angel.
The baby's on its way.

*Ballad
of the
Bread
Man*

*Charles
Causley
b. 1917*

Friends down under

Joseph was in the workshop
Planing a piece of wood.
The old man's past it, the neighbours said
That girl's been up to no good.

And who was that elegant feller,
They said, in the shiny gear?
The things they said about Gabriel
Were hardly fit to hear.

Mary never answered,
Mary never replied.
She kept the information,
Like the baby, safe inside.

It was election winter.
They went to vote in town.
When Mary found her time had come
The hotels let her down.

The baby was born in an annex
Next to the local pub.
At midnight, a delegation
Turned up from the Farmers' Club.

They talked about an explosion
That cracked a hole in the sky,
Said they'd been sent to the Lamb & Flag
To see God come down from on high.

A few days later a bishop
And a five-star general were seen
With the head of an African country
In a bullet-proof limousine.

We've come, they said, with tokens
For the little boy to choose.
Told the tale about war and peace
In the television news.

After them came the soldiers
With rifle and bomb and gun,
Looking for enemies of the state.
The family had packed and gone.

When they got back to the village
The neighbours said, to a man,
That boy will never be one of us,
Though he does what he blessed well can.

He went round to all the people
A paper crown on his head.
Here is some bread from my father.
Take, eat, he said.

Nobody seemed very hungry.
Nobody seemed to care.
Nobody saw the god in himself
Quietly standing there.

He finished up in the papers.
He came to a very bad end.
He was charged with bringing the living to life.
No man was that prisoner's friend.

There's only one kind of punishment
To fit that kind of a crime.
They rigged a trial and shot him dead.
They were only just in time.

They lifted the young man by the leg,
They lifted him by the arm,
They locked him in a cathedral
In case he came to harm.

They stored him safe as water
Under seven rocks.
One Sunday morning he burst out
Like a jack-in-the-box.

Through the town he went walking.
He showed them the holes in his head.
Now do you want any loaves? he cried.
Not today, they said.

Over to You

KITH AND KIN shows people closely known or related to each other. Here are some starting points for writing or talking. Many call for involvement in the situation presented by the poem, and some ask you to move out from there. Of course, there are many other approaches, and you will often have your own ideas for getting at the heart of the poem.

The One-Year-Old and *Baby Running Barefoot* show us babies as seen by adults. (i) How might adults appear to either baby? (ii) The babies meet: describe the meeting.

We Are Seven　(i) From the little girl's point of view tell in more detail of the deaths of the other children. (ii) The poet walks into the churchyard and ponders what he has seen and heard. What are his thoughts? (iii) From memory or imagination give a similar incident revealing a young child's innocence about death.

Our Father　(i) These children are talking in bed on a Saturday night. They think over the day and the day to come. Write some of their dialogue. (ii) The minister visits the mother to offer help but is rather surprised at her response. Write their conversation. (iii) Describe what the father is doing and thinking at some point in the middle of the week.

From 'The Family Reunion'　You are one of the children. Write your secret diary for a day in the holidays. (ii) Do the same for the first day after half-term. (iii) Would these children's opinion of their mother change when they themselves became parents?

Our Father, A Smell of Burning, From 'The Family Reunion' and *To My Mother* show four quite different mothers. Place them in order of preference, giving your ideas about good and bad mothers.

Puritan of the Pits　The poem is rich in details of this miner's life. Describe episodes in a documentary film set against this sort of background. You might try to illustrate such things as the miner's rugged individuality; the grown-up son's relationship with his father; a pit disaster; a whole way of life disappearing.

Blow the Candle Out　This poem needs music. Ideally you could work out your own tune, with guitar accompaniment. Or you could have the words spoken against some chords on the piano. Decide if a female voice would suit certain lines.
　The lovers meet, but is everything happy?

Arab Love Song   The girl, also awake, watches the night sky through her tent flap, thinking of her lover. In prose or verse try to catch something of her feelings.

Frankie and Johnnie   As with *Blow the Candle Out,* you might like to sing or accompany this ballad. Note the opportunities for a narrator and several performers. The poem is very dramatic and so could be turned into a play or short story.

Love and Marriage   (i) What are the prospects for this marriage? (The next poem, *After the Wedding,* may offer a helpful contrast.) Describe (ii) the man's feelings about his wife a few weeks after the wedding; (iii) the woman's feelings about the marriage two years later.

Her Husband   (i) As she keeps the food warm the wife wonders what her husband is doing. Describe the succession of pictures in her mind, giving the true facts where her imagination is astray. (ii) If the 'jurors' actually spoke, what might they say?

It's About Time and *What Almost Every Woman Knows Sooner or Later*   According to your sex (i) mention a few more points that might be added to the list of failings in either poem; (ii) defend your sex against some of the charges made.

Snapshots   (i) Add four or five more 'snapshots'. (ii) Give the listener's silent comments on some of the snapshots and on the whole occasion. (iii) Describe a few photographs of yourself at different ages that you would tear up if you could.

Ballad of the Bread Man   (i) Again you might like to bring in some music. It could possibly take the form of background music taped against a spoken version, but you would need to decide carefully on the tone of the poem and what music is appropriate. (ii) What would you say to a person who considered this poem blasphemous?

The section as a whole

(i) Some of the children in these poems are comparing notes about their parents. Write the conversation.

(ii) A parent from one of the poems has heard their talk, and joins in. What has he (or she) to say?

(iii) Magazines, films, singers and television have much to say about love – and some of the poems are also concerned with it. From these various fragments can you create a single picture of the nature of love?

(iv) Men and women seem to differ in temperament. What differences are suggested to you by any of the poems in the section?

(v) Write a story or poem starting with conflict or misunderstanding between relatives, friends or lovers. If it seems appropriate, end with reconciliation.

(vi) Some of the poems hint that we feel things about other people that we might not say. Write a dialogue between two people who know each other well, giving both words and (in brackets) thoughts and feelings.

Further Reading

You may wish to explore further some of the themes in the section. The possibilities are endless, but here are some suggestions.

(*Note:* In this and the subsequent reading lists the following symbols are used. Firstly, numbers denoting collections of verse, short stories and prose extracts as follows — some items are listed as appearing in various collections:

GENERAL ANTHOLOGIES

1   *Young Pegasus* I–V   Bell
2   *The Poet's Tongue*   Bell
3   *Poems for Pleasure*   III and IV   C.U.P.
4   *Sheldon Book of Verse* IV   O.U.P.

COLLECTIONS OF MODERN VERSE — a suggested basis for a small library

5   *Dawn and Dusk*   Brockhampton
6   *Rising Early*   Brockhampton
7   *Ten Contemporary Poets*   Harrap
8   *The Modern Poet's World*   Heinemann
9   *Here Today*   Hutchinson
10   *Nine Modern Poets*   Macmillan
11   *Poets of Our Time*   Murray
12   *Every Man Will Shout*   O.U.P.
13   *The New Poetry*   Penguin

MODERN SHORT STORIES AND PROSE EXTRACTS

14   *Chapters from the Modern Novel*   Bell
15   *A Choice of Modern Prose*   Bell
16   *A First Book of Modern Prose*   Cassell
17   *People and Diamonds*   C.U.P.
18   *Modern Short Stories*   Faber
19   *Thirteen Short Stories*   Longmans

Secondly, initials denoting publishers:

AR – Arnold; AU – Allen & Unwin; B – Blackie; C – C.U.P.; CA – Cape; CAS – Cassell; CO – Collier; COL – Collins; CON – Constable; COR – Corgi; CR – Cresset; CW – Chatto & Windus; D – Dent; DE – Deutsch; DU – Duckworth; E – Evans; F – Faber; FR – French; FS – Foursquare; G – Gollancz; H – Heinnemann; HD – Hart-Davis; HH – Hamish Hamilton; HRW – Holt, Rinehart & Winston; HU – Hutchinson; L – Longmans; M – Macmillan; ME – Methuen; MU – Murray; MUL – Muller; N – Nelson; NO –Nonesuch; O – O.U.P.; Os – O.U.P. Standard Authors; OD – Odhams; P – Penguin; PA – Pan; PEA – Peacock; PER – Pergamon; SJ – Sidgwick & Jackson; ULP – University of London Press; WHA – W. H. Allen.)

Poems dealing with childhood and youth are Blake's 'Piping Down the Valleys Wild', 'The Echoing Green', 'The Lamb', 'Infant Joy', 'Cradle Song', 'Nurse's Song' (Os); Lawrence's 'Baby Asleep After Pain' and 'Baby Song Ten Months Old' (*Poems :* H); Silkin's 'Death of a Child' (13); Causley's 'Timothy Winters' (9) and Betjeman's 'Indoor Games Near Newbury' (8). Mothers and motherhood are explored in Wordsworth: 'The Idiot Boy' (Os); R. Campbell: 'The Zulu Girl' (8); Cowper: 'On the Receipt of My Mother's Picture' (Os); Kavanagh: 'In Memory of My Mother' (7). Poems written by or about fathers are Wordsworth's 'Michael' (Os); Yeats's 'Prayer for My Son' and 'Prayer for My Daughter' (*Selected Poems :* M); Cummings' 'My Father Moved' (*Selected Poems :* F); Coleridge's 'Frost at Midnight' (Os) and Arnold's 'Sohrab and Rustum' (Os). Other family ties and the sense of the passing generations are the subject of 'Do Not Go Gentle' (D. Thomas: 10); 'The Great Grandmother' (Graves: 8); 'A Moment of Respect' (Brock: 9); 'The Drawer' (MacBeth: 9); 'The Prisoner of Chillon' (Byron: Os) and 'My Last Afternoon with Uncle Devereux Winslow' (Lowell: 12). Many ballads (as in *The Oxford Book of Ballads* and *English Poems and Ballads :* O) deal with both kith and kin. Of the uncountable poems concerned with other close relationships you may like to compare the following with those given: MacCaig: 'Particular You' (13); Frost: 'Love and a Question' (6); Auden: 'Lay Your Sleeping Head' (10); Larkin: 'Maiden Name' (10); Marvell: 'To His Coy Mistress' (4) and Hardy: 'The Contretemps' (*Selected Poems :* M).

Prose works depicting childhood in buoyant or adventurous mood are *Cider with Rosie* (Lee: P); *Heaven Lies About Us* (Spring: CON); *An Episode of Sparrows* (Godden: M); *Tom Sawyer* (Twain: N); 'A Conversation About Christmas' (D. Thomas in *A Prospect of the Sea :* D); *Village School* ('Miss Read': P); *My Early Life* (Churchill: OD, 15) and *Little Women* (Alcott: N). Works suggesting childhood or family difficulties are Lawrence: *Sons and Lovers* (P, 14); Dickens: *A Christmas Carol* (N); Joyce: *A Portrait of the Artist as a Young Man* (CA); Gosse *Father and Son* (H); Butler: *The Way of All Flesh* (D); A. Wilson: 'Raspberry Jam' (in *The Wrong Set :* P); Lawrence: *Second Best* (17); Waterhouse: *Billy Liar* (P); E. Brontë: *Wuthering Heights* (N); Steinbeck: *The Pearl* (H, P); and Spark: 'The Twins' (in *The Go-Away Bird :* P). *Clayhanger* (P) by Bennett surveys family life over a long period of time. The kinship of all people is elegantly asserted in Donne's Devotion XVII: 'Perchance he for whom this bell tolls' (NO).

Plays by nature are concerned with close relationships, but you might well enjoy reading, or better still, acting: Wilder: *Our Town* (L); Obey: *Noah* (H); Goldsmith: *She Stoops to Conquer* (L); Miller: *The Death of a Salesman* (P); Wesker: *Trilogy* (P); Rattigan: *The Winslow Boy* (L) – all very much concerned with family situations. *A Day in the Death of Joe Egg* (Nichols: F) deals with parental response to a retarded child, while contrasting pictures of marital 'triangles' are in *Candida* (Shaw: P) and *Look Back in Anger* (Osborne: F). Some useful situations for improvised drama are given in *The Group Approach to Drama* 1–3 (Adland: L).

II Strangers

The Tramp

John Clare
1793–1864

He eats (a moment's stoppage to his song)
The stolen turnip as he goes along;
And hops along and heeds with careless eye
The passing crowded stagecoach reeling by.
He talks to none, but wends his silent way,
And finds a hovel at the close of day,
Or under any hedge his house is made.
He has no calling and he owns no trade.
An old smoked blanket arches o'er his head,
A wisp of straw or stubble makes his bed.
He knows a lawless law that claims no kin
But meet and plunder on and feel no sin –
No matter where they go or where they dwell,
They dally with the winds and laugh at hell.

The Hermit

W. H. Davies
1871–1940

What moves that lonely man is not the boom
    Of waves that break against the cliff so strong;
Nor roar of thunder, when that travelling voice
    Is caught by rocks that carry far along.

'Tis not the groan of oak tree in its prime,
    When lightning strikes its solid heart to dust;
Nor frozen pond when, melted by the sun,
    It suddenly doth break its sparkling crust.

What moves that man is when the blind bat taps
    His window when he sits alone at night;
Or when the small bird sounds like some great beast
    Among the dead, dry leaves so frail and light.

Or when the moths on his night-pillow beat
    Such heavy blows he fears they'll break his bones;
Or when a mouse inside the papered walls,
    Comes like a tiger crunching through the stones.

One night when I went down
Thames' side, in London Town,
A heap of rags saw I,
And sat me down close by.
That thing could shout and bawl,
But showed no face at all;
When any steamer passed
And blew a loud shrill blast,
That heap of rags would sit
And make a sound like it;
When struck the clock's deep bell,
It made those peals as well.
When winds did moan around,
It mocked them with that sound.
When all was quiet, it
Fell into a strange fit;
Would sigh, and moan and roar,
It laughed, and blessed, and swore.
Yet that poor thing, I know,
Had neither friend nor foe;
Its blessing or its curse
Made no one better or worse.
I left it in that place –
The thing that showed no face.
Was it a man that had
Suffered till he went mad?
So many showers and not
One rainbow in the lot;
Too many bitter fears
To make a pearl from tears?

The
Heap
of Rags

W. H. Davies
1871–1940

After the disaster

The policeman buys shoes slow and careful; the teamster buys gloves slow and careful; they take care of their feet and hands; they live on their feet and hands.

The milkman never argues; he works alone and no one speaks to him; the city is asleep when he is on the job; he puts a bottle on six hundred porches and calls it a day's work; he climbs two hundred wooden stairways; two horses are company for him; he never argues.

The rolling-mill men and the sheet-metal men are brothers of cinders; they empty cinders out of their shoes after the day's work; they ask their wives to fix burnt holes in the knees of their trousers; their necks and ears are covered with a smut; they scour their necks and ears; they are brothers of cinders.

Psalm
of Those
Who Go
Forth

Carl Sandburg
b. 1878

*

The small porch of imitation
marble is never sunny, but
outside the front door he
sits on his kitchen chair facing
the street. In the bent yellowish
face, from under the brim
of a floppy brown hat,
his small eyes watch what
he is not living. But he
lives what he can:
watches without a smile, with
a certain strain, the warmth
of his big crumpled
body anxiously cupped
by himself in himself, as
he leans over himself not
over the cold railing, un-
moving but carefully getting
a little strength from the sight of the
passers-by. He has it
all planned: he will live
here morning by morning.

Taylor
Street

Thom Gunn
b. 1929

Song

John Clare
1793–1864

I peeled bits o strews and I got switches too
From the grey peeling Willow as Idlers do
And I switched at the flyes as I sat all alone
Till my flesh blood and marrow wasted to dry bone
My illness was love though I knew not the smart
But the beauty o love was the blood o my heart

Crowded places I shunned them as noises too rude
And flew to the silence of sweet solitude
Where the flower in green darkness, buds, blossoms and fades
Unseen of a shepherd and flower loving maids
The hermit bees find them but once and away
There I'll burry alive and in silence decay

I looked on the eyes o fair woman too long
Till silence and shame stole the use o my tongue
When I tried to speak to her I'd nothing to say
So I turned myself round and she wandered away
When she got too far off – why I'd something to tell
So I sent sighs behind her and talked to my sell

Willow switches I broke and I peeled bits and straws
Ever lonely in crowds in natures own laws
My ball room the pasture my music the Bees
My drink was the fountain my church the tall trees

Whoever would love or be tied to a wife
When it makes a man mad a' the days of his life

Eve's Lament

Anonymous
Fifteenth
Century

Alas, that ever that speche was spoken
    That the fals aungel seid to me!
Alas! oure maker's bidding is broken,
    For I have touched his owen dere tree.
Oure flescly eyn bin all unloken;
    Naked for sinne oureself we see;
That sory appel that we ham soken
    To dethe hathe brouth my spouse and me.

36

Unable to sleep I turn from the comfortless bed
And watch where the night turns all our roofs to metal;
The world's inhuman now and has its consequent peace.
I see you sadly asleep on the grateful sheets
That are for me ropes, knouts, hard instruments;
I am glad of these circumstances. It is not long
Since my deliberate savagery made you desperate
And you waited too long for any contrition at all.

When I pretend that the best words come in the dark
And you are asleep as I speak them to the deaf moon,
For such dishonesty the night rejects my fever
And the malevolent furniture sneers from its corners.

There was an old man of Kilcoo
to whom when he cared to name them
women came two by two
hoping he'd deign to tame them –
though he was chiefly bone,
badger-grey at the temples
and most of his top hair gone,
yet he might have been an archangel
the way that they carried on.

If he said 'Be off, you hussies!',
they'd avow that he had charm
and the hard words were roses.
So with one under each arm
he'd adjourn for recreation,
whose marrow had fed the seasons,
and they'd squabble him out of his reason
as to which should take precedence –
but the row would keep him warm:

The
Quarrel

Leslie Norris
b. 1921

The
Charmer

Alex Comfort
b. 1920

Until he'd picked a pair
that could talk like Scheherazade,
James Joyce and Poll the Parrot,
with knees that were cold and hard
and teeth that would serve a ferret
or have the leg off a chair –
to keep the others at bay –
though a nod from him would have had
the nicest, girl or married.

And there he was living in sin,
hell bent without the pleasure.
And we all saw what was coming
and the pickle that he was in –
till he cut the throats of the two.
So all his married neighbours
were sorry to see him hang –
grieved what it brought him to,
but still would have liked to learn
the way he had with women.

'Your father's gone,' my bald headmaster said.
His shiny dome and brown tobacco jar
Splintered at once in tears. It wasn't grief.
I cried for knowledge that was bitterer
Than any grief. For there and then I knew
That grief has uses – that a father dead
Could bind the bully's fist a week or two;
And then I cried for shame, then for relief.

I was a month past ten when I learnt this:
I still remember how the noise was stilled
In school-assembly when my grief came in.
Some goldfish in a bowl quietly sculled
Around their shining prison on its shelf.
They were indifferent. All the other eyes
Were turned towards me. Somewhere in myself
Pride, like a goldfish, flashed a sudden fin.

The Lesson

*Edward
Lucie-Smith
b. 1933*

n prison

Five O'Clock Shadow

John Betjeman
b. 1906

This is the time of day when we in the Men's Ward
    Think 'One more surge of the pain and I give up the fight',
When he who struggles for breath can struggle less strongly:
    This is the time of day which is worse than night.

A haze of thunder hangs on the hospital rose-beds,
    A doctors' foursome out on the links is played,
Safe in her sitting-room Sister is putting her feet up:
    This is the time of day when we feel betrayed.

Below the windows, loads of loving relations
    Rev in the car park, changing gear at the bend,
Making for home and a nice big tea and the telly:
    'Well, we've done what we can. It can't be long till the end.'

This is the time of day when the weight of bedclothes
    Is harder to bear than a sharp incision of steel.
The endless anonymous croak of a cheap transistor
    Intensifies the lonely terror I feel.

Dead Boys

Leslie
Norris
b. 1921

Here is the field, beneath two hundred houses,
Where the boy
Buried a dead bird.
He felt for it a small, universal sadness,
And gave it a birthday sixpence, all he had.
Among these urban gardens his remembered tears
Are old now, and real as the unravelling breezes
That thirty years blew all his griefs to dry.

The pond was here, its arid grains are laid
Higher than boys
About these flimsy garages.
All night long, all one long winter night,
The old tin Fords stood with their headlights turned
On its drowning ice, thin as a ripped sheet,
Where the covered slider lay in his silent bubbles
And would not be found. His school cap wrongly floated.

His name was known. The women sailed it
On gentle breath
Where they stood by the
Powerless cars in a darkness beyond rescue.
Gliding along in the cold of a frozen death
He had not realised, the boy in his eyeless sight
Saw the face of the drowned, and held it
For simple mourning. He heard the desperate

Cursing of helpless fathers as weak ice kept
Them impotent.
Days are long to a boy;
Nights buried his foundered sadness in their tides
Till the black hulks slept in softness, as he slept.
Once he was thoughtless to an easy friend. The roads
Of summer led them away and they broke in a rough moment,
Never to meet again. It was here that he said goodbye

To his angular childhood. He walks the streets,
Their garish doors
Open to the field long gone,
And the grown man smiles as returning he meets,
In his eyed love, the cold, immortal children.
They run unblighted the green lanes of their time,
They laugh, their bright innocence unknown around them;
Here, where the field was, they live, the dead boys.

The tall transformer stood
Biblically glorified, and then turned blue.
Space split. The earth tossed twelve hens in the air.
The landscape's hair stood up. The collie flew,
Or near it, back to the house and vanished there.

Roofed by a gravel pit,
I, in a safe place, as I always am,
Was, as I always am, observer only
– Not cared. Why should I? The belief's a sham
That shared danger or escape cures being lonely.

Struck
by
Lightning

Norman
MacCaig
b. 1911

41

Yet when I reached the croft
They excluded me by telling me. As they talked
Across my failure, I turned away to see
Hills spouting white and a huge cloud that walked
With a million million legs on to the sea.

The Rescue

Ted Hughes
b. 1930

That's what we live on: thinking of their rescue
And fitting our future to it. You have to see it:
First, the dry smudge above the sea-line,
Then the slow growth of a shipful of strangers
Into this existence. White bows, the white bow-wave
Cleaving the nightmare, slicing it open,
Letting in reality. Then all the sailors white
As maggots waving at the rail. Then their shouting –
Faintly at first, as you can think
The crowd coming with Christ sounded
To Lazarus in his cave.
Then the ship's horn giving blast after blast out
Announcing the end of the island. Then the rowboat.
I fancy I saw it happen. The five were standing
In the shallows with the deathly sea
Lipping their knees and the rattle of oar-locks
Shaking the sand out of their braincells,
The flash of wet oars slashing their eyes back alive –
All the time the long white liner anchoring the world
Just out there, crowded and watching.
Then there came a moment in the eternity of this island
When the row-boat's bows bit into the beach
And the lovely greetings and chatter scattered –
This is wrong.
        The five never moved.
They just stood sucked empty
As grasses by this island's silence. And the crew
Helped them into the boat not speaking
Knowing the sound of a voice from the world
Might grab too cheery-clumsy
Into their powdery nerves. Then they rowed off
Toward the shining ship with carefully

Hushed oars dipping and squeaking. And the five sat all the time
Like mummies with their bandages lifted off –
While the ship's dazzling side brimmed up the sky
And leaned over, pouring faces.

Two hours walk to work and back.
Rolling their eyes and rolling slightly,
Loose as runners on running tracks,
At dawn setting off, they return nightly
To where their shanty chimneys thrust
Blackened funnels from roofs of rust.
Over the saffron, smoke-smeared veld,
Braziers gleaming in mauve pink hollows,
Alexandra township's dust
Settles, as trilbies tilted, collars
Sodden, they slow up on the journey back.

Eight miles there and eight miles back.
Such exercise is beneficial,
Medical evidence is official
– though two hours walk on Kaffir beer,
Belching as the fortunate steer
Unsteady routes through blackleg cars
Offering lifts and opening doors
Usually closed, needs a clear
Motive to sustain the miles
Wearing down the twisted smiles.
Shoes in hand to save the leather,
At least they're certain of the weather
On the journey there and journey back.

Two hours there and two hours back.
Buses idle in their hangars,
Illustrate their only right,
To withhold custom from the white.
A penny busfare raise has proved
The straw upon the camel's back.
At check-points passes are demanded,
Holding them up along the track
Of this ballooning dream that severs

Bus
Boycott

Alan Ross
b. 1922

Economic links that bind
The victim to his servile grind.
Today will never be countermanded,
There cannot be a journey back.

Two hours there, and two hours back.
The glinting corrugated iron
Beckons in its smoking bowl,
Smells of mealie, smells of fear,
Which pedestrian workers share
With tsotsis on their evening prowl
For retribution – an apprehension lying
Like thunder in the sinking air.
Sweating sourly, each relying
On a corporative idea,
Follows his nose, and follows freely
His instinct there, his instinct back.

The Interrogation

Edwin
Muir
1887–1959

We could have crossed the road but hesitated.
And then came the patrol;
The leader conscientious and intent,
The men surly, indifferent.
While we stood by and waited
The interrogation began. He says the whole
Must come out now, who, what we are,
Where we have come from, with what purpose, whose
Country or camp we plot for or betray.
Question on question.
We have stood and answered through the standing day
And watched across the road beyond the hedge
The careless lovers in pairs go by,
Hand linked in hand, wandering another star,
So near we could shout to them. We cannot choose
Action or answer here,
Though still the careless lovers saunter by,
And the thoughtless field is near.
We are on the very edge,
Endurance almost done,
And still the interrogation is going on.

Nile Fishermen

Rex Warner
b. 1905

Naked men, fishing in Nile without a licence
kneedeep in it, pulling gaunt at stretched ropes.
Round the next bend is the police boat and the officials
ready to make an arrest on the yellow sand.

The splendid bodies are stark to the swimming sand,
taut to the ruffled water, the flickering palms,
yet swelling and quivering as they tug at the trembling ropes.
Their faces are bent along the arms and still.

Sun is torn in coloured petals on the water,
the water shivering in the heat and the north wind;
and near and far billow out white swollen crescents,
the clipping wings of feluccas, seagull sails.

A plunge in the turbid water, a quick joke stirs
a flashing of teeth, an invocation of God.
Here is food to be fetched and living from labour.
The tight ropes strain and the glittering backs for the haul.

Round the bend comes the police boat. The men scatter.
The officials blow their whistles on the golden sand.
They overtake and arrest strong bodies of men
who follow with sullen faces, and leave their nets behind.

Lamkin

Anonymous

It's Lamkin was a mason good
  As ever built wi' stane;
He built Lord Wearie's castle,
  But payment got he nane.

'O pay me, Lord Wearie,
  Come, pay to me my fee.'
'I canna pay you, Lamkin,
  For I maun gang o'er the sea.'

'O pay me now, Lord Wearie,
  Come, pay me out o' hand.'
'I canna pay you, Lamkin,
  Unless I sell my land.'

46

'O gin ye winna pay me,
    I here sall mak' a vow,
Before that ye come hame again,
    Ye sall hae cause to rue.'

Lord Wearie got a bonny ship,
    To sail the saut sea faem;
Bade his lady weel the castle keep,
    Ay till he should come hame.

'Gae bar the doors,' the lady said,
    'Gae well the windows pin;
And what care I for Lamkin
    Or any of his gang?'

But the nourice was a fause limmer   *limmer*: wretch
    As e'er hung on a tree;
She laid a plot wi' Lamkin,
    Whan her lord was o'er the sea.

She laid a plot wi' Lamkin,
    When the servants were awa',
Loot him in at a little shot-window,   *shot-window*:
    And brought him to the ha'.   window
                                             opening on
                                             a hinge
'O whare's a' the men o' this house,
    That ca' me the Lamkin?'
'They're at the barn-well thrashing;
    'Twill be lang ere they come in.'

'And whare's the women o' this house,
    That ca' me the Lamkin?'
'They're at the far well washing;
    'Twill be lang ere they come in.'

'And whare's the bairns o' this house,
    That ca' me the Lamkin?'
'They're at the school reading;
    'Twill be night or they come hame.'

'O whare's the lady o' this house,
    That ca's me the Lamkin?'
'She's up in her bower sewing,
    But we soon can bring her down.'

Then Lamkin's tane a sharp knife,
    That hung down by his gare,
And he has gi'en the bonny babe
    A deep wound and a sair.

gare : seam of skirt

The Lamkin he rockèd,
    And the fause nourice sang,
Till frae ilka bore o' the cradle
    The red blood out sprang.

bore : hole

Then out it spak' the lady,
    As she stood on the stair:
'What ails my bairn, nourice,
    That he's greeting sae sair?

greeting : wailing

'O still my bairn, nourice,
    O still him wi' the pap!'
'He winna still, lady,
    For this nor for that.'

'O still my bairn, nourice,
    O still him wi' the wand!'
'He winna still, lady,
    For a' his father's land.'

'O still my bairn, nourice,
    O still him wi' the bell!'
'He winna still, lady,
    Till ye come down yoursel'.'

O the firsten step she steppit,
    She steppit on a stane;
But the neisten step she steppit,
    She met him Lamkin.

'O mercy, mercy, Lamkin,
    Hae mercy upon me!
Though you hae ta'en my young son's life,
    Ye may let mysel' be.'

'O sall I kill her, nourice,
    Or sall I let her be?'
'O kill her, kill her, Lamkin,
    For she ne'er was good to me.'

48

'O scour the bason, nourice,
   And mak' it fair and clean,
For to keep this lady's heart's blood,
   For she's come o' noble kin.'

'There need nae bason. Lamkin,
   Lat it run through the floor;
What better is the heart's blood
   O' the rich than o' the poor?'

But ere three months were at an end,
   Lord Wearie came again;
But dowie, dowie was his heart   *dowie* : sorrowful
   When first he came hame.

'O wha's blood is this,' he says,
   'That lies in the cham'er?   *cham'er* : chamber
'It is your lady's heart's blood;
   'Tis as clear as the lamer.'   *lamer* : amber

'And wha's blood is this,' he says,
   That lies in my ha'?
It is your young son's heart's blood;
   'Tis the clearest ava'.'   *ava'* : of all

O sweetly sang the black-bird
   That sat upon the tree:
But sairer grat Lamkin,
   When he was condemn'd to dee.

And bonny sang the mavis
   Out o' the thorny brake;
But sairer grat the nourice,
   When she was tied to the stake.

A sight in camp in the daybreak gray and dim,
As from my tent I emerge so early sleepless,
As slow I walk in the cool fresh air the path near by the hospital tent,
Three forms I see on stretchers lying, brought out there untended lying,
Over each the blanket spread, ample brownish woollen blanket,
Gray and heavy blanket, folding, covering all.

Curious I halt and silent stand,
Then with light fingers I from the face of the nearest the first just lift the
    blanket;
Who are you elderly man so gaunt and grim, with well-gray'd hair, and
    flesh all sunken about the eyes?
Who are you my dear comrade?

Then to the second I step – and who are you my child and darling?
Who are you sweet boy with cheeks yet blooming?

Then to the third – a face nor child nor old, very calm, as of beautiful
    yellow-white ivory;
Young man I think I know you – I think this is the face of the Christ
    himself,
Dead and divine brother of all, and here again he lies.

It seemed that out of battle I escaped
Down some profound dull tunnel, long since scooped
Through granites which titanic wars had groined.
Yet also there encumbered sleepers groaned,
Too fast in thought or death to be bestirred.
Then, as I probed them, one sprang up, and stared
With piteous recognition in fixed eyes,
Lifting distressful hands as if to bless.
And by his smile, I knew that sullen hall,
By his dead smile I knew we stood in Hell.
With a thousand pains that vision's face was grained;
Yet no blood reached there from the upper ground,
And no guns thumped, or down the flues made moan.
'Strange friend,' I said, 'here is no cause to mourn.'
'None,' said the other, 'save the undone years,
The hopelessness. Whatever hope is yours,

A Sight in Camp

*Walt Whitman
1819–92*

Strange Meeting

*Wilfred Owen
1893–1918*

Was my life also; I went hunting wild
After the wildest beauty in the world,
Which lies not calm in eyes, or braided hair,
But mocks the steady running of the hour,
And if it grieves, grieves richlier than here.
For by my glee might many men have laughed,
And of my weeping something had been left,
Which must die now. I mean the truth untold,
The pity of war, the pity war distilled.
Now men will go content with what we spoiled.
Or, discontent, boil bloody, and be spilled.
They will be swift with swiftness of the tigress,
None will break ranks, though nations break from progress.
Courage was mine, and I had mystery,
Wisdom was mine, and I had mastery;
To miss the march of this retreating world
Into vain citadels that are not walled.
Then, when much blood had clogged their chariot-wheels
I would go up and wash them from sweet wells,
Even with truths that lie too deep for taint.
I would have poured my spirit without stint
But not through wounds; not on the cess of war.
Foreheads of men have bled where no wounds were.
I am the enemy you killed, my friend.
I knew you in this dark; for so you frowned
Yesterday through me as you jabbed and killed.
I parried; but my hands were loath and cold.
Let us sleep now . . .'

I Wake and Feel the Fell of the Dark

Gerard Manley
Hopkins
1844–89

I wake and feel the fell of the dark, not day.
What hours, O what black hours we have spent
This night! what sights you, heart, saw; ways you went!
And more must, in yet longer light's delay.
        With witness I speak this. But where I say
Hours I mean years, mean life. And my lament
Is cries countless, cries like dead letters sent
To dearest him that lives alas! away.
I am gall, I am heartburn. God's most deep decree
Bitter would have me taste: my taste was me;

Bones built in me, flesh filled, blood brimmed the curse.
Selfyeast of spirit a dull dough sours. I see
The lost are like this, and their scourge to be
As I am mine, their sweating selves; but worse.

*

SOUL: O who shall, from this Dungeon, raise
    A Soul inslav'd so many wayes?
    With bolts of Bones, that fetter'd stands
    In Feet; and manacled in Hands.
    Here blinded with an Eye; and there
    Deaf with the drumming of an Ear.
    A Soul hung up, as 'twere, in Chains
    Of Nerves, and Arteries, and Veins.
    Tortur'd, beside each other part,
    In a vain Head, and double Heart.

BODY: O who shall me deliver whole,
    From bonds of this Tyrannic Soul?
    Which, stretcht upright, impales me so,
    That mine own Precipice I go;
    And warms and moves this needless Frame:
    (A Fever could but do the same.)
    And, wanting where its spight to try,
    Has made me live to let me dye.
    A Body that could never rest,
    Since this ill Spirit it possest.

SOUL: What Magick could me thus confine
    Within anothers Grief to pine?
    Where whatsoever it complain,
    I feel, that cannot feel, the pain.
    And all my Care its self employes,
    That to preserve, which me destroys:
    Constrain'd not only to indure
    Diseases, but, whats worse, the Cure:
    And ready oft the Port to gain,
    Am Shipwrackt into Health again.

*A
Dialogue
Between
the Soul
and
Body*

*Andrew
Marvell
1621–78*

53

BODY: But Physick yet could never reach
  The Maladies Thou me dost teach;
  Whom first the Cramp of Hope does Tear:
  And then the Palsie Shakes of Fear.
  The Pestilence of Love does Heat:
  Or Hatred's hidden Ulcer eat.
  Joy's chearful Madness does perplex:
  Or Sorrow's other Madness vex.
  Which knowledge forces me to know;
  And Memory will not foregoe.
  What but a Soul could have the wit
  To build me up for Sin so fit?
  So Architects do square and hew,
  Green Trees that in the Forest grew.

Over to You

STRANGERS shows people separated from the world, from each other or from God. Most people suffer a sense of alienation at some time, and you may care to try writing poems on this theme. If prose comes more naturally to you – and this applies to most of the suggestions for writing – choose the medium which suits you.

The Tramp (i) Seeing the tramp, one of the travellers in the stagecoach starts condemning him, but another defends him. Write the conversation. (ii) The tramp starts thinking about his past life and why he became a tramp. Note the clues about his character in the poem and write his thoughts. (iii) How might the tramp's future turn out?

The Heap of Rags (i) What things have brought the 'heap of rags' to this condition? (ii) On a later occasion the speaker tries to help. What happens? (iii) In the afterlife, this 'loner' meets the two other dropouts, *The Tramp* and *The Hermit*. They compare their experiences on earth. Write some of the talk, conveying their nostalgia, regrets and other appropriate feelings.

Psalm of Those Who Go Forth Before Daybreak (i) Imagine you are the milkman: describe in more detail part of the round. (ii) Add two more sketches about people going early to work. (iii) A painter is attracted by some of the detail in this poem. After various experiments he gets to work on a large canvas. Describe some of his preliminary sketches and the layout of the finished work.

Taylor Street (i) The words 'live' and 'living' echo through the poem. Say (i) how the life of the sitter appears to one of the passers-by; (ii) how the sitter's past life appears to himself.

The Charmer Doubtless the old man provoked much chattering among the women of Kilcoo. As if for a tape-recording, write four or five snatches of their gossip. Include their comments on the hanging.

The Lesson (i) Describe a few moments in the boy's life on the day he hears the the news, including his walk to the headmaster's room. (ii) His friend recalls the next few days at school, including encounters with various other boys. What does he have to say?

Five O'Clock Shadow (i) The speaker looks round at some of his companions in the ward. Describe what he sees. (ii) Write snatches of the conversations heard round the bedsides at visiting time. (iii) Imagine or recall a stay in hospital where you felt lonely or abandoned. Sketch the scene in the ward and your feelings as you remember your normal healthy life.

The Rescue (i) The five people waiting to be rescued are compared with Lazarus and with mummies, the island with eternity. Imagine yourself to be one of the five and recall the last days or weeks on the island. (ii) Later you are interviewed for television. Give your version of the rescue and what followed on that day.

Bus Boycott In this poem of life in an African shanty-town a writer sees the germ of a television script. He sketches out a few sequences in which the walkers are set against their native background. Write up two of these sequences, dividing the material into Vision and Sound. Decide if your point of view should be sympathetic or detached. Include some conversation.

The Interrogation The interrogation is ended. Sketch the situation as it appears to (i) the 'careless lovers'; (ii) the speaker; (iii) the chief interrogator. It may help if you decide what country the incident is set in, but the people in the situation should be the focusing point.

Nile Fishermen Expand the poem into a short story which starts on the police boat and ends with wives or children collecting the abandoned nets. Note the photographic detail in the poem and include some in the story.

Lamkin (i) Most ballads were originally spoken, and a strong narrator (with perhaps some other voices for the speakers) could bring this poem alive for a small audience who were listening, not reading. (ii) A novelist decides to use this ballad as the basis of a story set in the *twentieth* century. Write two or three of the most dramatic incidents from the novel.

A Sight in Camp Perhaps you have seen pictures (even photographs) of the American Civil War. (i) Sketch the scene in and around the speaker's tent. (ii) Suggest what it is that has made the speaker restless. (iii) What circumstances might have brought the 'elderly man' and the 'sweet boy' to this pass? (iv) That night the speaker sleeps fitfully and imagines he hears the 'young man' speaking. Give his words.

A Sight in Camp and *Strange Meeting* An artist reads these two poems and sees them as two items in a large mural painting showing the pity of war. (i) Suggest how he might handle the two scenes in his picture. (ii) Mention another war poem you have read and explain how it too could inspire part of the picture.

A Dialogue Between the Soul and the Body You might appreciate the force of this fine poem by trying out different ways of reading the two 'parts', for example by having a deeper voice for the Body. If you were tape-recording, an echo-effect might suggest the soul. Could you devise a way of showing that though the Soul and Body are distinct, each speaks as though inextricably bound to the other?

The section as a whole

(i) 'We cannot understand each other, except in a rough and ready way; we cannot reveal ourselves, even when we want to' (E. M. Forster). Do the poems in Sections I and II (and your own experience) support or contradict these ideas?

ii) Which person in *Strangers* is the unhappiest? Why do you think so?

iii) Many of these poems show conflict and so could make the beginning of a story, play or film. Outline the plot and write the whole or part of such a work.

(iv) Write a dialogue between the person you are and the person others think you are.

(v) Sometimes in the theatre we see a series of tableaux illustrating a single theme. Choose a few of the poems in this section (or parts of poems) and suggest how they could be presented in such a way. You might consider the use of mime, masks, lighting, music, dance, audience participation, etc.

(vi) Which modern conditions make people strangers?

Further Reading *

You may have been impressed by the poems showing people who are strangers to the world or to others, and for comparison the following are suggested: D. Thomas: 'The Hunchback in the Park' (10, 12); E. Dickinson: 'I Heard a Fly Buzz when I Died' (8); Wordsworth: 'Resolution and Independence' (4); Yevtushenko: 'The Schoolmaster' (12); Tennyson: 'The Lady of Shalott' (1); De La Mare: 'The Listeners' (1); Betjeman: 'Death in Leamington' (10). A sense of detachment from humanity is seen in Larkin's 'Whitsun Weddings' (10, 13) and 'Mr Bleaney' (13) and in Auden's 'Who's Who' (8). 'The Men Who Wear My Clothes' (Scannell: 7) shows a man stranger to himself. Social divisions are seen in 'My Parents Kept Me' (Spender: 5, 10); 'Refugee Blues' (Auden: 8, 10); 'Mending a Wall' (Frost: 8); 'Dooley Is a Traitor' (Michie: 9) and, in an older setting, 'Hugh of Lincoln' (6). Some misalliances are examined in Auden's 'The Quarry' (5, 10); Eliot's 'The Love Song of J. Alfred Prufrock' (8); Blackburn's 'Cafe Talk' and 'A Small Keen Wind' (7); Scannell's 'They Did Not Expect This' (7); Browning's 'My Last Duchess' and 'Porphyria's Lover' (4) while Blake's 'The Garden of Love' (Os) provides a lyrical epitaph. Fear or hostility (sometimes sardonically expressed) is evident in 'The Poison Tree' (Blake: Os); 'Soliloquy in the Spanish Cloister' (Browning: 4); 'The Fear' (Frost: 12) and 'Get Up and Bar the Door' (1).

Young people in difficult relationships with others are depicted in *Childhood* by Gorki (C); 'The Goat and the Stars' by H. E. Bates (in *Short Stories since 1930* and in 16); the early chapters of *Oliver Twist* and *David Copperfield* by Dickens (P, N); *Lord of the Flies* by Golding (F, 14); *Jane Eyre* by C. Brontë (P, N); *Diary of a Young Girl* by A. Frank (HU, PA); *Catcher in the Rye* by Salinger (HH, P); *Shane* by Schaefer (H, PEA); *To Sir With Love* by Braithwaite (FS); *The Loneliness of the Long Distance Runner* by Sillitoe (PA, WHA); *Kipps* by Wells (COL); *Brighton Rock* by Greene (P); *Uncle Tom's Cabin* by H. B. Stowe (D) and *A Kind of Loving* by Barstow (P). Some individuals at odds with their group are seen in *The Autobiography of a Super Tramp* by W. H. Davies (AU); *Billy Budd* by Melville (D, P); *The Red Badge of Courage* by S. Crane (O, CO); *The Mayor of Casterbridge* by Hardy (M); *Lucky Jim* by Amis (P); *Silas Marner* by G. Eliot (P). Colour-bar difficulties are examined in Forster's *A Passage to India* (AR, P) and Paton's *Cry, the Beloved Country* (CA, P), while political events cause estrangements in *The Small Woman* (PA, 15) by Burgess and *The Grapes of Wrath* by Steinbeck (P, 14). Antagonisms great or subtle are seen in Guareschi: *The Little World of Don Camillo* (P); Hemingway: *The Battler* (17); Storey: *This Sporting Life* (15); Wain: *Hurry on Down* (P); Maugham: *The Luncheon* (19); O. Henry: *While the Auto Waits* (16); *The Ice Palace* (Fitzgerald: 18), and 'The Enemies' (D. Thomas in *A Prospect of the Sea*: D). Father and son are on different sides in Bret Harte's 'A Horseman in the

* For explanation of symbols see p. 30.

Sky' (in *Short Stories Old and New*: L). There is a fine tension also in Hardy's story 'The Three Strangers'. The customs of far-off peoples are well described in Melville's *Typee* (D) and Grimble's *A Pattern of Islands* (15) and *Return to the the Islands* (MU).

Drama is of course rich in conflicts of every sort. Many of Galsworthy's plays (DU), as their titles suggest (e.g. *Strife, The Skin Game*), show deep estrangements. A single person in conflict with a social or political group may be observed in *Saint Joan* (Shaw: P, L); *The Playboy of the Western World* (Synge: D); *A Man for All Seasons* (Bolt: H, FR); *The Crucible* (Miller: CR; MUL) and *Billy Liar* (Waterhouse: B). Difficult relationships are seen in *Pygmalion* (Shaw: P, L); *The Caucasian Chalk Circle* (Brecht: ME); *Juno and the Paycock* (O'Casey: M); *A View from the Bridge* (Miller: P) and *Romanoff and Juliet* (Ustinov: H). Failure to communicate is the essence of much of Pinter (e.g. *The Dumb Waiter*: P). Tensions among plotters are explored in *The July Plot* (Manvell: B). A collection dealing with trial scenes is *Drama in Court* (ed. Roberts: AR).

III Earth, Air, Fire and Water

Millom Old Quarry

Norman Nicholson b. 1914

'They dug ten streets from that there hole,' he said,
'Hard on five hundred houses.' He nodded
Down the set of the quarry and spat in the water
Making a moorhen cock her head
As if a fish had leaped. 'Half the new town
Came out of yonder – King Street, Queen Street, all
The houses round the Green as far as the slagbank,
And Market Street, too, from the Crown allotments
Up to the Station Yard.' – 'But Market Street's
Brown freestone,' I said. 'Nobbut the facings;
We called them the Khaki Houses in the Boer War,
But they're Cumberland slate at the back.'

I thought of those streets still bearing their royal names
Like the coat-of-arms on a child's Jubilee Mug –
Nonconformist gables sanded with sun
Or branded with burning creeper; a smoke of lilac
Between the blue roofs of closet and coal-house:
So much that woman's blood gave sense and shape to
Hacked from this dynamited combe.
The rocks cracked to the pond, and hawthorns fell
In waterfalls of blossom. Shed petals
Patterned the scum like studs on the sole of a boot,
And stiff-legged sparrows skid down screes of gravel.

I saw the town's black generations
Packed in their caves of rock, as mussel or limpet
Washed by the tidal sky; then swept, shovelled
Back in the quarry again, a landslip of lintels
Blocking the gape of the tarn.
The quick turf pushed a green tarpaulin over
All that was mortal in five thousand lives.
Nor did it seem a paradox to one
Who held quarry and query, turf and town,
In the small lock of a recording brain.

60

John Henry

Anonymous

When John Henry was a little fellow,
   You could hold him in the palm of your hand,
He said to his pa, 'When I grow up
   I'm gonna be a steel-driving man.
     Gonna be a steel-driving man.'

When John Henry was a little baby,
   Setting on his mammy's knee,
He said, 'The Big Bend Tunnel on the C. & O. Road
 Is gonna be the death of me,
    Gonna be the death of me.'

One day his captain told him,
   How he had bet a man
That John Henry would beat his steam drill down,
   Cause John Henry was the best in the land,
   John Henry was the best in the land.

John Henry kissed his hammer
   White man turned on steam,
Shaker held John Henry's trusty steel,
   Was the biggest race the world had ever seen,
    Lord, biggest race the world ever seen.

John Henry on the right side,
   The steam drill on the left,
'Before I'll let your steam drill beat me down,
   I'll hammer my fool self to death,
    Hammer my fool self to death.'

Captain heard a mighty rumbling,
   Said, 'The mountain must be caving in,'
John Henry said to the captain,
   'It's my hammer swinging in de wind,
    My hammer swinging in de wind.'

John Henry said to his shaker,
   'Shaker, you'd better pray;
For if ever I miss this piece of steel,
   Tomorrow'll be your burial day,
    Tomorrow'll be your burial day.'

John Henry said to his captain,
   'Before I ever leave town,
Gimme a twelve-pound hammer wid a whale-bone handle,
   And I'll hammer dat steam driver down,
     I'll hammer dat steam drill on down.'

John Henry said to his captain,
   'A man ain't nothin' but a man,
But before I'll let dat steam drill beat me down
   I'll die wid my hammer in my hand,
     Die wid my hammer in my hand.'

The man that invented the steam drill
   He thought he was mighty fine,
John Henry drove down fourteen feet,
   While the steam drill only made nine,
     Steam drill only made nine.

'Oh, lookaway over yonder, captain,
   You can't see like me,'
He gave a long and loud and lonesome cry,
   'Lawd, a hammer be the death of me!
     A hammer be the death of me!'

John Henry hammering on the mountain
   As the whistle blew for half-past two,
The last words his captain heard him say,
   'I've done hammered my insides in two,
     Lawd, I've hammered my insides in two.'

The hammer that John Henry swung
   It weighed over twelve pound,
He broke a rib in his left hand side
   And his intrels fell on the ground,
     And his intrels fell on the ground.

John Henry, O, John Henry,
   His blood is running red,
Fell right down with his hammer to the ground,
   Said, 'I beat him to the bottom but I'm dead,
     Lawd, beat him to the bottom but I'm dead.'

When John Henry was laying there dying,
   The people all by his side,
The very last words they heard him say,
   'Give me a cool drink of water 'fore I die,
     Cool drink of water 'fore I die.'

John Henry had a little woman,
   The dress she wore was red,
She went down the track, and she never looked back,
   Going where her man fell dead,
     Going where her man fell dead.

They carried him down by the river,
   And buried him in the sand,
And everybody that passed that way,
   Said, 'There lies that steel-driving man,
     There lies a steel-driving man.'

They took John Henry to the river,
   And buried him in the sand,
And every locomotive come a-roaring by,
   Says, 'There lies that steel-drivin' man,
     Lawd, there lies a steel-driving man.'

Some say he came from Georgia,
   And some from Alabam,
But it's wrote on the rock at the Big Bend Tunnel,
   That he was an East Virginia man,
     Lord, Lord, an East Virginia man.

When you destroy a blade of grass
You poison England at her roots:
Remember no man's foot can pass
Where evermore no green life shoots.

You force the birds to wing too high
Where your unnatural vapours creep:
Surely the living rocks shall die
When birds no rightful distance keep.

You have brought down the firmament
And yet no heaven is more near;
You shape huge deeds without event,
And half-made men believe and fear.

Your worship is your furnaces,
Which, like old idols, lost obscenes,
Have molten bowels; your vision is
Machines for making more machines.

O, you are busied in the night,
Preparing destinies of rust;
Iron misused must turn to blight
And dwindle to a tetter'd crust.

The grass, forerunner of life, has gone,
But plants that spring in ruins and shards
Attend until your dream is done:
I have seen hemlock in your yards.

The generations of the worm
Know not your loads piled on their soil;
Their knotted ganglions shall wax firm
Till your strong flagstones heave and toil.

When the old hollow'd earth is crack'd,
And when, to grasp more power and feasts,
Its ores are emptied, wasted, lack'd,
The middens of your burning beasts

Shall be raked over till they yield
Last priceless slags for fashionings high,
Ploughs to wake grass in every field,
Chisels men's hands to magnify.

To
Iron-Founders
and
Others

Gordon
Bottomley
1874–1948

Earthquake

Cleator
Moor

Norman
Nicholson
b. 1914

From one shaft at Cleator Moor
They mined for coal and iron ore.
This harvest below ground could show
Black and red currants on one tree.

In furnaces they burnt the coal,
The ore was smelted into steel,
And railway lines from end to end
Corseted the bulging land.

Pylons sprouted on the fells,
Stakes were driven in like nails,
And the ploughed fields of Devonshire
Were sliced with the steel of Cleator Moor.

The land waxed fat and greedy too,
It would not share the fruits it grew,
And coal and ore, as sloe and plum,
Lay black and red for jamming time.

The pylons rusted on the fells,
The gutters leaked beside the walls,
And women searched the ebb-tide tracks
For knobs of coal or broken sticks.

But now the pits are wick with men,
Digging as dogs dig for a bone:
For food and life *we* dig the earth –
In Cleator Moor they dig for death.

Every wagon of cold coal
Is fire to drive a turbine wheel;
Every knuckle of soft ore
A bullet in a soldier's ear.

The miner at the rockface stands,
With his segged and bleeding hands
Heaps on his head the fiery coal,
And feels the iron in his soul.

Too far for you to see
The fluke and the foot-rot and the fat maggot
Gnawing the skin from the small bones,
The sheep are grazing at Bwlch-y-Fedwen,
Arranged romantically in the usual manner
On a bleak background of bald stone.

Too far for you to see
The moss and the mould on the cold chimneys,
The nettles growing through the cracked doors,
The houses stand empty at Nant-yr-Eira,
There are holes in the roofs that are thatched with sunlight,
And the fields are reverting to the bare moor.

Too far, too far to see
The set of his eyes and the slow phthisis
Wasting his frame under the ripped coat,
There's a man still farming at Ty'n-y-Fawnog,
Contributing grimly to the accepted pattern,
The embryo music dead in his throat.

R. S. Thomas
b. 1913

Beleaguered
Cities

Build your houses, build your houses, build your towns,
   Fell the woodland, to a gutter turn the brook,
Pave the meadows, pave the meadows, pave the downs,
   Plant your bricks and mortar where the grasses shook,
   The wind-swept grasses shook.
Build, build your Babels black against the sky —
But mark yon small green blade, your stones between,
   The single spy
Of that uncounted host you have outcast;
For with their tiny pennons waving green
   They shall storm your streets at last.

Build your houses, build your houses, build your slums,
   Drive your drains where once the rabbits used to lurk,
Let there be no song there save the wind that hums
   Through the idle wires while dumb men tramp to work,
   Tramp to their idle work.

F. L. Lucas
1894–1967

Water everywhere

Silent the siege; none notes it; yet one day
Men from your walls shall watch the woods once more
  Close round their prey.
Build, build the ramparts of your giant-town;
Yet they shall crumble to the dust before
  The battering thistle-down.

Bulkeley, Hunt, Willard, Hosmer, Meriam, Flint,
Possessed the land which rendered to their toil
Hay, corn, roots, hemp, flax, apples, wool and wood.
Each of these landlords walked amidst his farm,
Saying, ''Tis mine, my children's and my name's.
How sweet the west wind sounds in my own trees!
How graceful climb those shadows on my hill!
I fancy these pure waters and the flags
Know me, as does my dog: we sympathise;
And, I affirm, my actions smack of the soil.'

Where are these men? Asleep beneath their grounds:
And strangers, fond as they, their furrows plough.
Earth laughs in flowers, to see her boastful boys
Earth-proud, proud of the earth which is not theirs;
Who steer the plough, but cannot steer their feet
Clear of the grave.
They added ridge to valley, brook to pond,
And sighed for all that bounded their domain;
'This suits me for a pasture; that's my park;
We must have clay, lime, gravel, granite ledge,
And misty lowland, where to go for peat.
The land is well, – lies fairly to the south.
'Tis good, when you have crossed the sea and back,
To find the sitfast acres where you left them.'
Ah! the hot owner sees not Death, who adds
Him to his land, a lump of mould the more.
Hear what the earth says: –

Hamatreya*

*Ralph Waldo
Emerson
1803–82*

* *Hamatreya :*
Earth-mother

EARTH SONG

'Mine and yours;
Mine, not yours.
Earth endures;
Stars abide –
Shine down in the old sea;
Old are the shores;
But where are the old men?
I who have seen much,
Such have I never seen.

'The lawyer's deed
Ran sure,
In tail,
To them, and to their heirs
Who shall succeed,
Without fail,
Forevermore.

'Here is the land,
Shaggy with wood,
With its old valley,
Mound and flood.
But the heritors? –
Fled like the flood's foam.
The lawyer, and the laws,
And the kingdom,
Clean swept herefrom.

'They called me theirs,
Who so controlled me;
Yet every one
Wished to stay, and is gone;
How am I theirs,
If they cannot hold me,
But I hold them?'

When I heard the Earth-song
I was no longer brave;
My avarice cooled
Like lust in the chill of the grave.

The winged bull trundles to the wired perimeter.
Cumbrously turns. Shivers, brakes clamped,
Bellowing four times, each engine tested
With routine ritual. Advances to the runway.
Halts again as if gathering heart
Or warily snuffing for picador cross-winds.
Then, then, a roar open-throated.
Affronts the arena. Then fast, faster
Drawn by the magnet of his *idée fixe*,
Head down, tail up, he's charging the horizon.
   And the grass of the airfield grows smooth as a fur.
The runway's elastic and we the projectile;
Installations control-tower mechanics parked aeroplanes –
Units all woven to a ribbon unreeling,
Concrete melts and condenses to an abstract
Blur, and our blood thickens to think of
Rending, burning, as suburban terraces
Make for us, wave after wave.
                        The moment
Of Truth is here. We can only trust,
Being as wholly committed to other hands
As a babe at birth, Europa to the bull god.
And as when one dies in his sleep, there's no divining
The instant of take-off, so we who were earth-bound
Are air-borne, it seems, in the same breath.
The neutered terraces subside beneath us.

   Bank and turn, bank and turn,
Air-treading bull, my silver Alitalia!
Bank and turn, while the earth below
Swings like a dial on the wing-tip's axis,
Whirls and checks like a wheel of chance!
Now keep your course! On azure currents
Let the wings lift and sidle drowsily –
A halcyon rocked by the ghost of the gale.
To watchers in Kent you appear as a quicksilver
Bead skimming down the tilted sky;
To the mild-eyed aircrew, an everyday office:
To us, immured in motion, you mean
A warm womb pendant between two worlds.
   O trance prenatal and angelic transport!
Like embryos curled in this aluminium belly –
Food and oxygen gratis – again
We taste the pure freedom of the purely submissive.

The passive dominion of the wholly dependent.
Through heaven's transparent mysteries we travel
With a humdrum of engines, the mother's heartbeat:
And our foreshadowed selves begin to take shape, to be
Dimly adapted to their destination.
What migrant fancies this journeying generates! –
Almost we imagine a metempsychosis.

   Over the Channel now, beneath the enchanting
Inane babble of a baby-blue sky,
We soar through cloudland, at the heights of nonsense.
From a distance they might be sifted-sugar-drifts,
Meringues, iced cakes, confections of whipped cream
Lavishly piled for some Olympian party –
A child's idea of heaven. Now radiant
All around the airscrew's boring penumbra
The clouds redouble, as nearer we climb,
Their toppling fantasy. We skirt the fringe of icebergs,
Dive under eiderdowns, disport with snowmen
On fields of melting snow dinted by the wind's feet,
Gleefully brush past atom-bomb cauliflowers,
Frozen fuffs of spray from naval gunfire.
   Wool-gathering we fly through a world of make-believe.
We *are* the aircraft, the humming-bird hawk moth
Hovering and sipping at each cloud corolla;
But also ourselves, to whom these white follies are
Valid as symbols for a tonic reverie
Or as symptoms of febrile flight from the real.
Let us keep, while we can, the holiday illusion,
The heart's altimeter dancing bliss-high,
Forgetting gravity, regardless of earth
Out of sight, out of mind, like a menacing letter
Left at home in a drawer – let the next-of-kin acknowledge it.

   The cloud-floor is fissured suddenly. Clairvoyance
It seems, not sight, when the solid air frays and parts
Unveiling, like some rendezvous remote in a crystal,
Bright, infinitesimal, a fragment of France.
We scan the naked earth as it were through a skylight:
Down there, what life-size encounters, what industrious
Movement and vocations manifold go forward!
But to us, irresponsible, above the battle,
Villages and countryside reveal no more life than
A civilization asleep beneath a glacier,

Toy bricks abandoned on a plain of linoleum . . .
    After a hard winter, on the first warm day
The invalid venturing out into the rock-garden,
Pale as a shaft of December sunshine, pauses,
All at sea among the aubretia, the alyssum
And arabis – halts and moves on how warily,
As if to take soundings where the blossom foams and tumbles:
But what he does sound is the depth of his own weakness
At last, as never when pain-storms lashed him.
So we, convalescent from routine's long fever,
Plummeting our gaze down to river and plain,
Question if indeed that dazzling world beneath us.
Be truth or delirium; and finding still so tentative
The answer, can gauge how nearly we were ghosts,
How far we must travel yet to flesh and blood.

    But now the engines have quickened their beat
And the fuselage pulsates, panting like a fugitive.
Below us – oh, look at it! – earth has become
Sky, a thunderscape curdling to indigo,
Veined with valleys of green fork-lightning.
The atrocious Alps are upon us. Their ambush –
A primeval huddle, then a bristling and heaving of
Brutal boulder-shapes, an uprush of Calibans –
Unmasks its white-fanged malice to maul us.
The cabin grows colder. Keep height, my angel!
    Recall how flyers from a raid returning,
Lightened of one death, were elected for another:
Their homing thoughts too far ahead, a mountain
Stepped from the mist and slapped them down.
We, though trivial the hazard, retract
Our trailing dreams until we have cleared these ranges.
Exalted, numinous, aloof no doubt
To the land-locked vision, for us they invoke
A mood more intimate, a momentary flutter and
Draught of danger – death's fan coquettishly
Tapping the cheek ere she turn to dance elsewhere.
Our mien is the bolder for this mild flirtation,
Our eyes the brighter, since every brush with her
Gives flesh a souvenir, a feel of resurrection.

Those peaks o'erpassed, we glissade at last to
A gentian pasture, the Genoan sea.
Look south, sky-goers! In flying colours
A map's unrolled there – the Italy
Your schooldays scanned once: the hills are sand-blond,
A pale green stands for the littoral plain:
The sea's bedizened with opening islands
Like iris eyes on a peacock's fan.
How slowly dawns on the drowsy newborn
Whose world's unwon yet – a firelit dress,
An ego's glamorous shell, a womb of rumours –
The first faint glimmering of otherness!
But half awake, we could take this country
For some vague drift from prenatal dreams:
Those hills and headlands, like sleep's projections
Or recollections, mere symbol seem.
    Then hurtling southward along shores of myrtle,
Silverly circle the last lap,
My bull-headed moth! This land is nothing
But a mythical name on an outline map
For us, till we've scaled it to our will's dimensions,
Filled in each wayward, imperious route,
Shaded it in with delays and chagrins,
Traced ourselves over it, foot by foot.
Now tighter we circle, as if the vertical
Air is a whirlpool drawing us down;
And the airfield, a candle-bright pinpoint, invites us
To dance ere alighting . . Hurry! We burn
For Rome so near us, for the phoenix moment
When we have thrown off this traveller's trance,
And mother-naked and ageless-ancient
Wake in her warm nest of renaissance.

An Irish Airman Foresees His Death

William Butler Yeats 1865–1939

I know that I shall meet my fate
Somewhere among the clouds above;
Those that I fight I do not hate,
Those that I guard I do not love;
My country is Kiltartan Cross,
My countrymen Kiltartan's poor,
No likely end could bring them loss
Or leave them happier than before.
Nor law, nor duty bade me fight,
Nor public men, nor cheering crowds,
A lonely impulse of delight
Drove to this tumult in the clouds;
I balanced all, brought all to mind,
The years to come seemed waste of breath,
A waste of breath the years behind
In balance with this life, this death.

*

London Snow

Robert Bridges 1844–1930

When men were all asleep the snow came flying,
In large white flakes falling on the city brown,
Stealthily and perpetually settling and loosely lying,
     Hushing the latest traffic of the drowsy town;
Deadening, muffling, stifling its murmurs failing;
Lazily and incessantly floating down and down:
     Silently sifting and veiling road, roof, and railing;
Hiding difference, making unevenness even,
Into angles and crevices softly drifting and sailing.
     All night it fell, and when full inches seven
It lay in the depth of its uncompacted lightness,
The clouds blew off from a high and frosty heaven;
     And all woke earlier for the unaccustomed brightness
Of the winter dawning, the strange unheavenly glare:
The eye marvelled – marvelled at the dazzling whiteness;
     The ear hearkened to the stillness of the solemn air;
No sound of wheel rumbling nor of foot falling,
And the busy morning cries came thin and spare.
     Then boys I heard, as they went to school, calling,
They gathered up the crystal manna to freeze
Their tongues with tasting, their hands with snowballing;
Or rioted in a drift, plunging up to the knees;

Or peering up from under the white-mossed wonder,
'O look at the trees!' they cried, 'O look at the trees!'
  With lessened load a few carts creak and blunder,
Following along the white deserted way,
A country company long dispersed asunder:
  When now already the sun, in pale display
Standing by Paul's high dome, spread forth below
His sparkling beams, and awoke the stir of the day.
  For now doors open, and war is waged with the snow,
And trains of sombre men, past tale of number,
Tread long brown paths, as toward their toil they go:
  But even for them awhile no cares encumber
Their minds diverted; the daily word is unspoken,
The daily thoughts of labour and sorrow slumber
At the sight of the beauty that greets them, for the charm they have
    broken.

Sun, wild October sun, unleash your lions.
Send them from brazen Africa, let them lean
Into my garden. (Even at night I know of
Those definite fences; there is deep slinking
Behind the water butt.)
Let them ignite the garage, let them enter
The house, leaving their yellow spoor
On the carpets. Let them invade my eyes,
I shall cage them behind my lashes.
Look, all the windows of my house are opened outwards,
Look, my eyes are open.

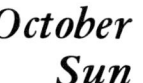

*October
Sun*

Leslie Norris
b. 1921

After I got religion and steadied down
They gave me a job in the canning works,
And every morning I had to fill
The tank in the yard with gasoline,
That fed the blow-fires in the sheds
To heat the soldering irons.
And I mounted a rickety ladder to do it,
Carrying buckets full of the stuff.

*Butch
Weldy*

Edgar Lee
Masters
1869–1950

77

One morning, as I stood there pouring,
The air grew still and seemed to heave,
And I shot up as the tank exploded,
And down I came with both legs broken,
And my eyes burned crisp as a couple of eggs.
For someone left a blow-fire going,
And something sucked the flame in the tank.
The Circuit Judge said whoever did it
Was a fellow servant of mine, and so
Old Rhodes' son didn't have to pay me.
And I sat on the witness stand as blind
As Jack the Fiddler, saying over and over,
'I didn't know him at all.'

Never until the mankind making
Bird beast and flower
Fathering and all humbling darkness
Tells with silence the last light breaking
And the still hour
Is come of the sea tumbling in harness

And I must enter again the round
Zion of the water bead
And the synagogue of the ear of corn
Shall I let pray the shadow of a sound
Or sow my salt seed
In the least valley of sackcloth to mourn

The majesty and burning of the child's death.
I shall not murder
The mankind of her going with a grave truth
Nor blaspheme down the stations of the breath
With any further
Elegy of innocence and youth.

Deep with the first dead lies London's daughter,
Robed in the long friends,
The grains beyond age, the dark veins of her mother,
Secret by the unmourning water
Of the riding Thames.
After the first death, there is no other.

A Refusal to Mourn the Death, by Fire, of a Child in London

Dylan Thomas
1914–53

Don't You Smell Fire?

Thomas Hood
1799–1845

Run! – run for St Clement's engine!
  For the Pawnbroker's all in a blaze,
And the pledges are frying and singeing –
  Oh! how the poor pawners will craze!
Now where can the turncock be drinking?
  Was there ever so thirsty an elf? –
But he still may tope on, for I'm thinking
  That the plugs are as dry as himself.

The engines! – I hear them come rumbling;
  There's the Phoenix! the Globe! and the Sun!
What a row that will be, and a grumbling,
  When the water don't start for a run!
See! there they come racing and tearing,
  All the street with loud voices is fill'd;
Oh! it's only the firemen a-swearing
  At a man they've run over and kill'd!

How sweetly the sparks fly away now,
  And twinkle like stars in the sky;
It's a wonder the engines don't play now,
  But I never saw water so shy!
Why, there isn't enough for a snipe,
  And the fire it is fiercer, alas!
Oh! instead of the New River pipe,
  They have gone – that they have – to the gas!

Only look at the poor little P—'s
  On the roof – is there anything sadder?
My dears, keep fast hold, if you please,
  And they won't be an hour with the ladder!
But if anyone's hot in their feet,
  And in very great haste to be saved,
Here's a nice easy bit in the street,
  That McAdam has lately unpaved!

There is some one – I see a dark shape
  At that window, the hottest of all, –
My good woman, why don't you escape?
  Never think of your bonnet and shawl:
If your dress isn't perfect, what is it
  For once in a way to your hurt?
When your husband is paying a visit
  There, at Number Fourteen, in his shirt!

Only see how she throws out her *chaney*!
  Her basins, and teapots, and all
The most brittle of *her* goods – or any,
  But they all break in breaking their fall:
Such things are not surely the best
  From a two-storey window to throw –
She might save a good iron-bound chest,
  For there's plenty of people below!

Oh dear! what a beautiful flash!
  How it shone through the window and door;
We shall soon hear a scream and a crash,
  When the woman falls thro' with the floor!
There! there! what a volley of flame,
  And then suddenly all is obscured! –
Well – I'm glad in my heart that I came; –
  But I hope the poor man is insured!

Out of a fired ship, which, by no way
But drowning, could be rescued from the flame,
Some men leap'd forth, and ever as they came
Neere the foes ships, did by their shot decay;
So all were lost, which in the ship were found,
They in the sea being burnt, they in the burnt ship drown'd.

A Burnt Ship

John Donne
1572–1631

It moved so slowly, friendly as a dog
Whose teeth would never bite;
It licked the hand with cool and gentle tongue
And seemed to share its parasites' delight
Who moved upon its back or moored among
The hairy shallows overhung
With natural parasols of leaves
And bubbling birdsong.
Ukuleles twanged and ladies sang
In punts and houseboats vivid as our own
Bold paintings of the Ark;

A Day on the River

Vernon
Scannell
b. 1922

This was summer's self to any child:
The plop and suck of water and the old
Sweet rankness in the air beguiled
With deft archaic spells the dim
Deliberations of the land,
Dear river, comforting
More than the trailing hand.

The afternoon of sandwiches and flasks
Drifted away
The breeze across the shivering water grew
Perceptibly in strength.
The sun began to bleed.
'Time to go home,' the punctured uncles said,
And back on land
We trembled at the river's faint, low growl
And as birds probed the mutilated sky
We knew that, with the night,
The river's teeth grew sharp
And they could bite.

On a Friend's Escape from Drowning off the Norfolk Coast

George Barker
b. 1913

Came up that cold sea at Cromer like a running grave
    Beside him as he struck
Wildly towards the shore, but the blackcapped wave
    Crossed him and swung him back,
And he saw his son digging in the castled dirt that could save.
    Then the farewell rock
Rose a last time to his eyes. As he cried out
    A pawing gag of the sea
Smothered his cry and he sank in his own shout
    Like a dying airman. Then she
Deep near her son asleep on the hourglass sand
    Was awakened by whom
Save the Fate who knew that this was the wrong time:
    And opened her eyes
On the death of her son's begetter. Up she flies
    Into the hydra-headed

Grave as he closes his life upon her who for
    Life has so richly bedded him.
But she drove through his drowning like Orpheus and tore
    Back by the hair
Her escaping bridegroom. And on the sand their son
    Stood laughing where
He was almost an orphan. Then the three lay down
    On that cold sand,
Each holding the other by a living hand.

The sheets were frozen hard, and they cut the naked hand;
The decks were alike a slide, where a seaman scarce could stand;
The wind was a nor'wester, blowing equally off the sea;
And cliffs and spouting breakers were the only things a-lee.

They heard the surf a-roaring before the break of day;
But 'twas only with the peep of light we saw how ill we lay.
We tumbled every hand on deck instanter, with a shout,
And we gave her the maintops'l, and stood by to go about.

All day we tacked and tacked between the South Head and the North;
All day we hauled the frozen sheets, and got no further forth;
All day as cold as charity, in bitter pain and dread,
For very life and nature we tacked from head to head.

We gave the South a wider berth, for there the tide-race roared;
But every tack we made we brought the North Head close aboard:
So's we saw the cliffs and houses, and the breakers running high,
And the coastguard in his garden, with his glass against his eye.

The frost was on the village roofs as white as ocean foam;
The good red fires were burning bright in every 'longshore home;
The windows sparkled clear, and the chimneys volleyed out;
And I vow we sniffed the victuals as the vessel went about.

Christmas at Sea

Robert Louis
Stevenson
1850–94

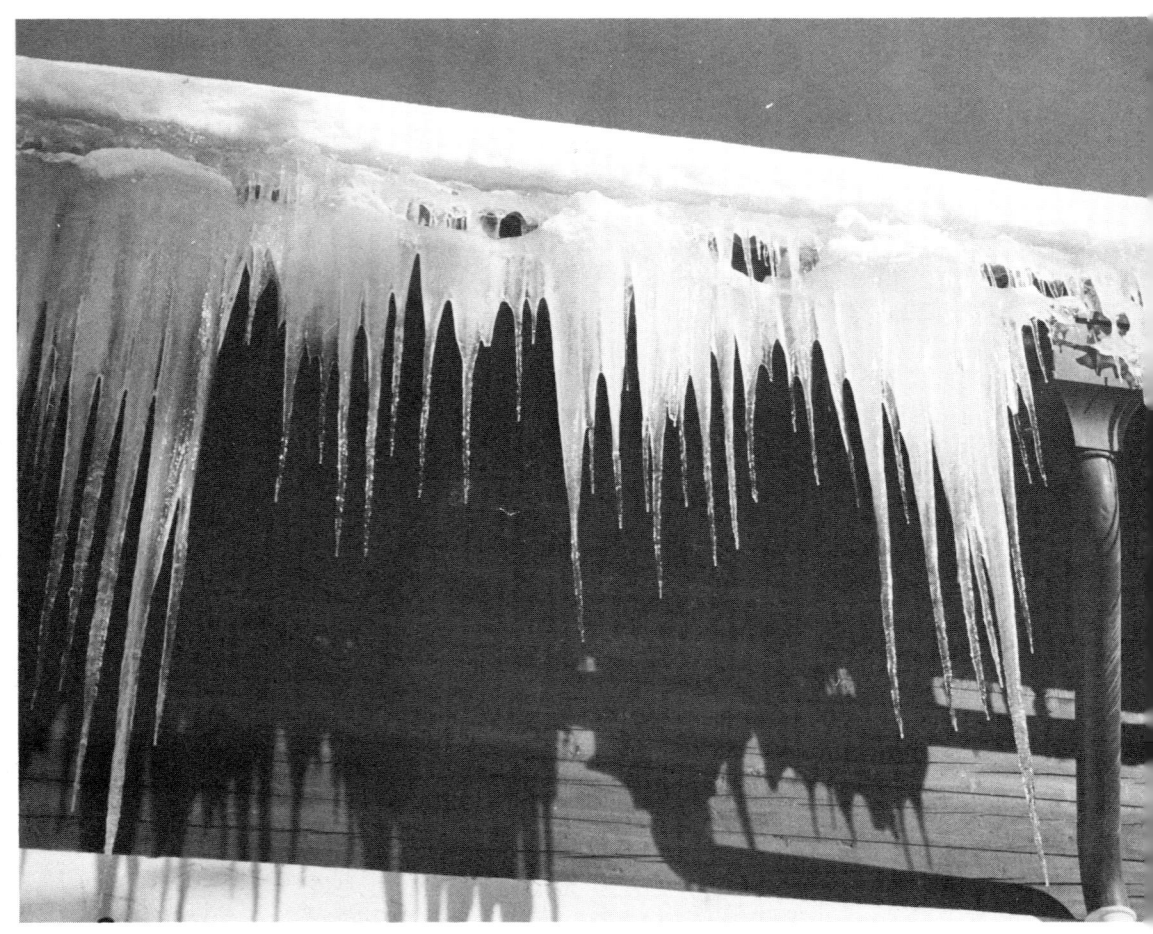

Icicles

The bells upon the church were rung with a mighty jovial cheer;
For it's just that I should tell you how (of all days in the year)
This day of our adversity was blessèd Christmas morn,
And the house above the coastguard's was the house where I was born.

O well I saw the pleasant room, the pleasant faces there,
My mother's silver spectacles, my father's silver hair;
And well I saw the firelight, like a flight of homely elves,
Go dancing round the china-plates that stand upon the shelves.

And well I knew the talk they had, the talk that was of me,
Of the shadow on the household and the son that went to sea;
And O the wicked fool I seemed, in every kind of way,
To be here and hauling frozen ropes on blessèd Christmas Day.

They lit the high sea-light, and the dark began to fall.
'All hands to loose topgallant sails,' I heard the captain call.
'By the Lord, she'll never stand it,' our first mate, Jackson cried.
. . . 'It's the one way or the other, Mr Jackson,' he replied.

She staggered to her bearings, but the sails were new and good,
And the ship smelt up to windward just as though she understood.
As the winter's day was ending, in the entry of the night,
We cleared the weary headland, and passed below the light.

And they heaved a mighty breath, every soul on board but me,
As they saw her nose again pointing handsome out to sea;
But all that I could think of, in the darkness and the cold,
Was just that I was leaving home and my folks were growing old.

The Con-vergence of the Twain

Thomas Hardy
1840–1928

In a solitude of the sea,
        Deep from human vanity,
And the pride of Life that planned her, stilly couches she.

        Steel chambers, late the pyres
        Of her salamandrine fires,
Cold currents thrid, and turn to rhythmic tidal lyres.

        Over the mirrors meant
        To glass the opulent
The sea-worm crawls – grotesque, slimed, dumb, indifferent.

        Jewels in joy designed
        To ravish the sensuous mind
Lie lightless, all their sparkles bleared and black and blind.

        Dim moon-eyed fishes near
        Gaze at the gilded gear
And query: 'What does this vaingloriousness down here?' . . .

        Well: while was fashioning
        This creature of cleaving wing,
The Immanent Will that stirs and urges everything

        Prepared a sinister mate
        For her, so gaily great –
A Shape of Ice, for the time far and dissociate.

        And as the smart ship grew
        In stature, grace and hue,
In shadowy silent distance grew the Iceberg too.

        Alien they seemed to be:
        No mortal eye could see
The intimate welding of their later history,

        Or sign that they were bent
        By paths coincident
On being anon twin halves of one august event,

        Till the Spinner of the Years
        Said 'Now!' And each one hears,
And consummation comes, and jars two hemispheres.

Over to You

Though science and technology have given man increasing control over his environment he is still very much aware of the natural forces around him. EARTH, AIR, FIRE AND WATER shows us poets in different moods responding to the elements or contemplating them in a philosophical way.

Millom Old Quarry   The poet locks his impressions in his 'recording brain', but a friend wishes to take away a visual impression. He takes some photographs of local people and their background. Describe some of these and give the captions he puts beneath them.

John Henry   (i) Read the poem aloud a few times, with speakers for John Henry, the Captain and the people, and a quiet chorus for the last line of each verse. (ii) The Shaker tells the story, years later. Give his version. (iii) Tell a story or write a ballad about another man competing with a machine.

Cleator Moor   A miner is talking about past and present. He compares the days of the Slump (verse 5) with the present need to produce the raw materials for war (verses 6, 7 and 8). Write some of what he says.

To Iron-Founders and Others, Cleator Moor and *Beleaguered Cities* are protesting in different ways about man's assault on nature. In the manner of a Counsel for the Defence, plead the case against these complaints. (The end of the first of the three poems might give you a starting point.)

The Welsh Hill Country   A ciné camera pans first over a wide sweep of the hill country, then changes to close-ups of details not mentioned by the poet. What appears on the screen in each case?

Hamatreya   Read and discuss the poem, and write your ideas on how it might be presented by a group. Consider the use of individual voices, male and female, choruses, music and other sound effects. Decide whether any visual interest (costumes, episcope projections, etc.) would help.

Flight to Italy   Notice the powerful effects of the poet's images (the 'air-treading bull' and the 'embryo curled in this aluminium belly' are important ones). With these as flashpoints, describe two other parts of the journey, for example the plane passing over a town, river or forest.

London Snow   (i) A very young child and a very old man look out on the snowy scene. Say what each sees, hears and feels. (ii) Describe the journey to work of one of the 'sombre men'.

Butch Weldy   (i) Give an observer's account of the minutes immediately after the accident. (ii) In dialogue form give an excerpt from the court proceedings mentioned near the end of the poem. Make clear the nature of the case. (iii)

Say whether or not Butch Weldy's religion might have helped him to accept his misfortune.

Don't You Smell Fire? (i) Did you find that the poem succeeded in being funny in spite of the subject? (ii) Make a list of grim subjects which *could* be written about humorously, and another of those which could or should not. If possible attempt one from your first list.

A Burnt Ship (i) After discussion of and perhaps research into former sea-battles, describe the deaths of two men, one in the ship and one in the sea. (ii) What does the poem suggest to you about the poet? (iii) The preceding four poems show people suffering from fire. Write a poem or piece of prose dealing with the magic or excitement of fire. It might help to compare the early days of fire with, say, a Bonfire Night blaze.

A Day on the River One night the boy returns to the river and rows across it. Describe what he sees and feels as daytime and night-time impressions mingle.

On a Friend's Escape from Drowning (i) In what ways might a film show the horror of the incident? (Remember the three people concerned and the possible use of flashback.) (ii) Look up the legends of the Hydra and of Orpheus and write two other modern incidents to parallel them.

Christmas at Sea Write the radio version of the incident which alternates between the ship and houses. (ii) The tailpiece of the programme is a narrative. In it the storyteller recalls the relief of the crew contrasting with his own depression. Write the script.

– The section as a whole

(i) The last five poems show water as an enemy. Write an imaginative piece in which water is recognised as a friend.

(ii) For which three or four of the people in these poems have you most sympathy?

(iii) Find a newspaper account which roughly parallels the theme of one of the poems. Compare the impact each makes upon you.

(iv) Which 'element' seems the most fruitful source of poetry? Why should this be?

(v) Some topics not included in the section are Potholing, Spaceflight, Forest Fire, Undersea Exploration. From experience or imagination write a poem or prose piece on one of these.

(vi) Write a short radio script for four voices: Earth, Air, Fire, Water. Some of the poems in the section may suggest ideas. In appropriate parts the voices could be heard together.

Further Reading *

If you enjoyed this section you have touched a rich vein. Much poetry, especially modern, shows man in some kind of opposition to the elements. The stubbornness of the soil is well conveyed by the poems of R. S. Thomas (e.g. 'Enigma' (7), 'A Peasant' (7, 13), 'Welsh Landscape' (7, 10, 11, 13), 'The Labourer' and 'Soil' (10). Poems of mining are 'A Ballad of a Mine' (R. Skelton: 6) and 'The Collier' (Watkins: 5). Earth is seen in hostile form in Owen's 'Futility' (8, 10); Dunlop's 'Landscape as Werewolf' (9) and Kirkup's 'Earthquake' (11). Man's response to air and wind is felt in 'Breathless' (Noyce: 12); 'A Windy Day' (Young: 8); 'Wind' (T. Hughes: 13); 'Ode to the West Wind' (Shelley: 4); 'Landscape Near an Aerodrome' (Spender: 4, 3); 'London to Paris by Air' (Gorell: 3) and 'Sing We the Two Lieutenants' (Day Lewis: 2). Destructive fire is the subject of 'Some Verses Upon the Burning of Our House' (Anne Bradstreet in *American Poetry*: Harper & Row); 'Incendiary' (Scannell: 7) and 'The Casualty' (T. Hughes: 12). Water (sometimes in its icier forms) has attracted the attention of most poets, for example Cowley: 'Drinking' (4); Rossetti: 'The White Ship' (Os); Wordsworth: extract from 'The Prelude' (2); Ingelow: 'The High Tide on the Coast of Lincolnshire' (2); Masefield: 'Sea Fever' (1); Fry: 'Rain on Dry Ground' (12); Kirkup: 'The Submerged Village' (11); A. Ross: 'Survivors' (11); P. Dickinson: 'The Dam' (11); Muir: 'Ballad of the Flood' (6, 11); Eliot: 'The Dry Salvages' (10, F); Lawrence: 'A Snowy Day at School' (*Collected Poems*: H); F. Thompson: 'To a Snowflake' (Os).

A good prose account of the collier's life is 'Down the Mine' (Orwell in *Selected Essays*: P) which you might read in conjunction with Chapter 3 of *The Road to Wigan Pier* (same author and publisher). Spencer Chapman's *Living Dangerously* (CW) and Hunt's *Ascent of Everest* (ULP) deal with mountaineering, while Scott's *Last Expedition* (MU, 15) and *The Crossing of Antarctica* (Fuchs and Hillary: CAS) give accounts of Polar exploration. Many books give a strong sense of terrain, e.g. Bates: *The Purple Plain* (N); Meade Faulkner: *Moonfleet* (AR); and Hardy's *The Return of the Native* (M). *The Last Days of Pompeii* (Lytton: COL) will remind us of earth's hidden anger. The terror of wind is vividly described in Chapter 55 of *David Copperfield* (Dickens: N, P) and *A High Wind in Jamaica* (R. Hughes: CW, FS); while Clostermann's *Flames in the Sky* (CW) and Bates' *Fair Stood the Wind for France* (P) deal with the hazards of flying. Fire in action is dealt with in Chapter 8 of *The History of Mr Polly* (Wells: COL); *Old St Paul's* Ainsworth: N) and Pepys' *Diary* for 1666, 2–7 September (N). An interesting comparison with Hardy's poem on the Titanic is provided by *A Night to Remember* (Lord: HRW). Other sea mishaps are in *Lord Jim* (Conrad: P) and *Fire at Sea* (Gallagher: PA), and various sea adventures will be found in *The Old Man and the Sea* (Hemingway: CA); *The Cruel Sea* (Monsarrat: PA); *The Kon-tiki*

* For explanation of symbols see p. 30.

Expedition (Heyerdahl: P); *Mr Midshipman Hornblower* (Forrester: P); *Twenty Thousand Leagues Under the Sea* (Verne: D); *Saga of the Sea* (Ed. Jones and Rose: L) and *Nautilus 90 North* (Anderson: N). Much gentler exploits are described in Jerome's *Three Men in a Boat* (D).

A few plays related in theme to the items given are: *The Price of Coal* (Brighouse in *Nine Modern Plays*: N); a dramatic version of Verne's *Twenty Thousand Leagues* (in *May We Recommend*, Bk. VI: L); *On Board the Golden Hind* (in *Seven Modern Plays*: N); *Treasure Island* (Connell: B); *Christopher Columbus* (Louis MacNeice: F); and *The Caine Mutiny* in *Drama in Court* (Roberts: AR). Synge's *Riders to the Sea* shows the sea taking its toll of the men of a family.

IV Other Kingdom

I think I could turn and live awhile with the animals . . . they are so
    placid and self-contained,
I stand and look at them sometimes half the day long.

They do not sweat and whine about their condition,
They do not lie awake in the dark and weep for their sins,
They do not make me sick discussing their duty to God,
Not one is dissatisfied . . . not one is demented with the mania of
    owning things,
Not one kneels to another nor to his kind that lived thousands of years
    ago,
Not one is respectable or industrious over the whole earth.

I Think
I Could
Turn and
Live

Walt Whitman
(from 'Song of
Myself')
1819–92

here's a little mouse)and
what does he think about, i
wonder as over this
floor(quietly with

bright eyes)drifts(nobody
can tell because
Nobody knows, or why
jerks Here &, here,
gr(oo)ving the room's Silence) this like
a littlest
poem a
(with wee ears and see?

tail frisks)
        (gonE)
'mouse',
      We are not the same you and

here's a
little
mouse

e. e. cummings
1894–1962

i, since here's a little he
or is
it It
?   (or was something we saw in the mirror)?

therefore we'll kiss; for maybe
what was Disappeared
into ourselves
who   (look).   , startled

Dog

Alexander Reid
b. 1914

He sets no limit on his admiration,
His love is absolute and truly blind.
He lives in ecstasies of adoration
And deifies the least of humankind.

All that we do is beautiful and right
In his soft eyes and though the word grieves,
Is all unearned, he bows his head contrite
And lacking understanding, he believes.

The Jaguar

Ted Hughes
b. 1930

The apes yawn and adore their fleas in the sun.
The parrots shriek as if they were on fire, or strut
Like cheap tarts to attract the stroller with the nut.
Fatigued with indolence, tiger and lion

Lie still as the sun. The boa-constrictor's coil
Is a fossil. Cage after cage seems empty, or
Stinks of sleepers from the breathing straw.
It might be painted on a nursery wall.

But who runs like the rest past these arrives
At a cage where the crowd stands, stares, mesmerised,
As a child at a dream, at a jaguar hurrying enraged
Through prison darkness after the drills of his eyes

On a short fierce fuse. Not in boredom –
The eye satisfied to be blind in fire,
By the bang of blood in the brain deaf the ear –
He spins from the bars, but there's no cage to him

More than to the visionary his cell:
His stride is wildernesses of freedom:
The world rolls under the long thrust of his heel.
Over the cage floor the horizons come.

*

Harassed Creatures

   Yet by the unclouded sun are hourly bred
The bold assailants that surround thine head,
Poor patient Ball! and with insulting wind
Roar in thine ears, and dart the piercing sting:
In thy behalf the crest-waved boughs avail
More than thy short-clipt remnant of a tail,
A moving mockery, a useless name,
A living proof of cruelty and shame.
Shame to the man, whatever fame he bore,
Who took from thee what man can ne'er restore,
Thy weapon of defence, thy chiefest good,
When swarming flies contending suck thy blood.
Nor thine alone the suffering, thine the care,
The fretful Ewe bemoans an equal share;
Tormented into sores, her head she hides,
Or angry brushes from her new-shorn sides.
Penned in the yard, e'en now at closing day
Unruly Cows with marked impatience stay,
And vainly striving to escape their foes,
The pail kick down; a piteous current flows.

*Robert
Bloomfield
(from 'The
Farmer's Boy')
1766–1823*

93

I came across her browsing on a slope
Thatched with dry brown fern scythed in a day
Between milkings, the stones hid in each clump
Blunting the brush-hooks' blades, clanging back
Unhuman oaths over the hill's shoulder
In a noon crackling with summer's fierce wit.
There, mooning and nosing about the grass-tops
Chaffed with holocausts of laughing flame
Or full of chuckling juice mellow as mead,
With an inward jolt at sudden confrontation
She looked up fixedly with liquid eyes
Wide as the stretch of innocence that holds
Pellets of gamin treachery, eyes full of
Remorseless motherhood and blind foraging,
With her two stomachs quite outwitting love,
Lust even, in the common faith
Of bull and cowdom: tyranny of gut.
Being on the loose for laughs, I ran at her
And watched her bolt, all belly and backside
With teats like bagpipes slung beneath a bronco,
For she exploded then, a milk-filled grenade
Gone careering down the slope to others
Watching her progress with the same wet eyes
Till off they all went, down the hill together,
Horns down, hoofs up, harridans gone dancing
Hell for leather; and, as much a part of the dance,
Centaur wise I followed in the wake
Of the heifers, leaping down those summer slopes,
Laughing, shouting, mad with the fun of it all.

Mark how the feathered tenants of the flood,
With grace of motion that might scarcely seem
Inferior to angelical, prolong
Their curious pastime! shaping in mid air
(And sometimes with ambitious wing that soars
High as the level of the mountain-tops)
A circuit ampler than the lake beneath –
Their own domain; but ever, while intent
On tracing and retracing that large round,

Cow Dance

Bruce Beaver
b. 1928

Waterfowl

William
Wordsworth
1770–1850

oomed buffalo

Their jubilant activity evolves
Hundreds of curves and circlets, to and fro,
Upward and downward, progress intricate
Yet unperplexed, as if one spirit swayed
Their indefatigable flight. 'Tis done –
Ten times, or more, I fancied it had ceased;
But lo! the vanished company again
Ascending; they approach – I hear their wings,
Faint, faint at first; and then an eager sound,
Past in a moment – and as faint again!
They tempt the sun to sport amid their plumes;
They tempt the water, or the gleaming ice,
To show them a fair image; 'tis themselves,
Their own fair forms, upon the glimmering plain,
Painted more soft and fair as they descend
Almost to touch – then up again aloft,
Up with a sally and a flash of speed,
As if they scorned both resting-place and rest!

The Heron

Vernon
Watkins
1906–67

The cloud-backed heron will not move:
He stares into the stream.
He stands unfaltering while the gulls
And oyster-catchers scream.
He does not hear, he cannot see
The great white horses of the sea,
But fixes eyes on stillness
Below their flying team.

How long will he remain, how long
Have the grey woods been green?
The sky and the reflected sky,
Their glass he has not seen,
But silent as a speck of sand
Interpreting the sea and land,
His fall pulls down the fabric
Of all that windy scene.

Sailing with clouds and woods behind,
Pausing in leisured flight,
He stepped, alighting on a stone,
Dropped from the stars of night.
He stood there unconcerned with day,
Deaf to the tumult of the bay,
Watching a stone in water,
A fish's hidden light.

Sharp rocks drive back the breaking waves,
Confusing sea with air.
Bundles of spray blown mountain-high
Have left the shingle bare.
A shipwrecked anchor wedged by rocks,
Loosed by the thundering equinox,
Divides the herded waters,
The stallion and his mare.

Yet no distraction breaks the watch
Of that time-killing bird.
He stands unmoving on the stone;
Since dawn he has not stirred.
Calamity about him cries,
But he has fixed his golden eyes
On water's crooked tablet,
On light's reflected word.

Time was when I was free as air,
The thistle's downy seed my fare,
    My drink the morning dew;
I perch'd at will on ev'ry spray,
My form genteel, my plumage gay,
    My strains for ever new.

But gawdy plumage, sprightly strain,
And form genteel, were all in vain,
    And of a transient date;
For, caught and cag'd, and starv'd to death,
In dying sighs my weary breath
    Soon pass'd the wiry grate.

On a
Goldfinch
Starved
to Death
in His Cage

William
Cowper
1731–1800

Dragon fish

Sea horse

Thanks, gentle swain, for all my woes,
And thanks for this effectual close
    And cure of ev'ry ill!
More cruelty none could express;
And I, if you had shown me less,
    Had been your pris'ner still.

I caught this morning morning's minion, king-
    dom of daylight's dauphin, dapple-dawn-drawn Falcon, in his riding
    Of the rolling level underneath him steady air, and striding
High there, how he rung upon the rein of a wimpling wing
In his ecstasy! then off, off forth on swing,
    As a skate's heel sweeps smooth on a bow-bend: the hurl and gliding
    Rebuffed the big wind. My heart in hiding
Stirred for a bird, – the achieve of, the mastery of the thing!

Brute beauty and valour and act, oh, air, pride, plume, here
    Buckle! AND the fire that breaks from thee then, a billion
Times told lovelier, more dangerous, O my chevalier!

    No wonder of it: sheer plod makes plough down sillion
Shine, and blue-bleak embers, ah my dear,
    Fall, gall themselves, and gash gold-vermilion.

The Wind-hover

To Christ our Lord

Gerard Manley Hopkins 1844–99

As Jupiter's all-seeing eye
Survey'd the worlds beneath the sky,
From this small speck of earth were sent
Murmurs and sounds of discontent;
For ev'ry thing alive complain'd
That he the hardest life sustain'd.
    Jove calls his Eagle. At the word
Before him stands the royal bird.
The Bird, obedient, from heav'n's height
Downward directs his rapid flight;

The Eagle, and the Assembly of Animals

John Gay 1685–1732

Then cited ev'ry living thing,
To hear the mandates of his king.
   'Ungrateful creatures, whence arise
These murmurs which offend the skies;
Why this disorder? say the cause:
For just are Jove's eternal Laws.
Let each his discontent reveal.
To yon sour dog I first appeal.'
   'Hard is my lot,' the hound replys.
'On what fleet nerves the greyhound flys!
While I with weary step and slow
O'er plains and vales and mountains go;
The morning sees my chase begun,
Nor ends it 'till the setting sun.'
   'When' (says the greyhound) 'I pursue,
My game is lost, or caught in view,
Beyond my sight the prey's secure:
The hound is slow but always sure.
And, had I his sagacious scent,
Jove ne'er had heard my discontent.'
   The lyon crav'd the foxe's art;
The fox, the lyon's force and heart;
The cock implor'd the pidgeon's flight,
Whose wings were rapid, strong and light;
The pidgeon strength of wing despis'd,
And the cock's matchless valour priz'd:
The fishes wish'd to graze the plain,
The beasts to skim beneath the main.
Thus, envious of another's state,
Each blam'd the partial hand of Fate.
   The bird of heav'n then cry'd aloud.
'Jove bids disperse the murm'ring croud:
The God rejects your idel prayers.
Would ye, rebellious mutineers,
Entirely change your name and nature,
And be the very envy'd creature?
What, silent all, and none consent!
Be happy then, and learn content.
Nor imitate the restless mind,
And proud ambition of mankind.'

A white-hot midday in the Snake Park.
Lethargy lay here and there in coils,
And here and there a neat obsidian head
Lay dreaming on a plaited yellow pillow of its own
Loops like a pretzel or a true-love-knot.

A giant python seemed a heap of tyres;
Two Nielsen's Vipers looked for a way out,
Sick of their cage and one another's curves;
And the long Ringsnake brought from Lembuland
Poured slowly through an opening like smoke.

Leaning intently forward a young girl
Discerned in stagnant water on a rock
A dark brown shoestring or discarded whiplash,
Then read the label to find out the name,
Then stared again: it moved. She screamed.

Old Piet Rander leant with us that day
On the low wall around the rocky space
Where amid broken quartz that cast no shade
Snakes twitched or slithered, or appeared to sleep
Or lay invisible in the singing glare.

The sun throbbed like a fever as he spoke:
'Look carefully at this shrub with glossy leaves.'
Leaves bright as brass. 'That leaf on top
Just there, do you see that it has eyes?
That's a Green Mamba, and it's watching *you*.

'A man I once knew did survive the bite,
Saved by a doctor running with a knife,
Serum and all. He was never the same again.
Vomiting blackness, agonising, passing blood,
Part paralysed, near gone, he felt

'(He told me later) he would burst apart;
But the worst agony was in his mind –
Unbearable nightmare, worse than total grief
Or final loss of hope, impossibly magnified
To a blind person of panic and extreme distress.'

*William
Plomer
b. 1903*

'Why should that little head have power
To inject all horror for no reason at all?'
'Ask me another – and beware of snakes.'
The sun was like a burning-glass. Face down
The girl who screamed had fallen in a faint.

Lizards and Snakes

Anthony Hecht
b. 1923

On the summer road that ran by our front porch
    Lizards and snakes came out to sun.
It was hot as a stove out there, enough to scorch
    A buzzard's foot. Still, it was fun
To lie in the dust and spy on them. Near but remote,
    They snoozed in the carriage ruts, a smile
In the set of the jaw, a fierce pulse in the throat
Working away like Jack Doyle's after he'd run the mile.

Aunt Martha had an unfair prejudice
    Against them (as well as being cold
Towards bats.) She was pretty inflexible in this,
    Being a spinster and all, and old.
So we used to slip them into her knitting box.
    In the evening she'd bring in things to mend
And a nice surprise would slide out from under the socks.
It broadened her life, as Joe said. Joe was my friend.

But we never did it again after the day
    Of the big wind when you could hear the trees
Creak like rockingchairs. She was looking away
    Off, and kept saying, 'Sweet Jesus, please
Don't let him near me. He's as like as twins.
    He can crack us like lice with his fingernail.
I can see him plain as a pikestaff. Look how he grins
And swinges the scaly horror of his folded tail.'

I caught a tremendous fish
and held him beside the boat
half out of water, with my hook
fast in a corner of his mouth.
He didn't fight.
He hadn't fought at all.
He hung a grunting weight,
battered and venerable
and homely. Here and there
his brown skin hung in strips
like ancient wall-paper:
shapes like full-blown roses
stained and lost through age.
He was speckled with barnacles,
fine rosettes of lime,
and infested
with tiny white sea-lice,
and underneath two or three
rags of green weed hung down.
While his gills were breathing in
the terrible oxygen
– the frightening gills,
fresh and crisp with blood,
that can cut so badly –
I thought of the coarse white flesh
packed in like feathers,
the big bones and the little bones,
the dramatic reds and blacks
of his shiny entrails,
and the pink swim-bladder
like a big peony.
I looked into his eyes
which were far larger than mine
but shallower, and yellowed,
the irises backed and packed
with tarnished tinfoil
seen through the lenses
of old scratched isinglass.
They shifted a little, but not
to return my stare.
– It was more like the tipping
of an object toward the light.
I admired his sullen face,
the mechanism of his jaw,

The
Fish

*Elizabeth
Bishop
b. 1911*

and then I saw
that from his lower lip
– if you could call it a lip –
grim, wet, and weapon-like,
hung five old pieces of fish-line,
or four and a wire leader
with the swivel still attached,
with all their five big hooks
grown firmly in his mouth.
A green line, frayed at the end
where he broke it, two heavier lines,
and a fine black thread
still crimped from the strain and snap
when it broke and he got away.
Like medals with their ribbons
frayed and wavering,
a five-haired beard of wisdom
trailing from his aching jaw.
I stared and stared
and victory filled up
the little rented boat,
from the pool of bilge
where oil had spread a rainbow
around the rusted engine
to the bailer rusted orange,
the sun-cracked thwarts,
the oarlocks on their strings,
the gunnels – until everything
was rainbow, rainbow, rainbow!
And I let the fish go.

igeons shelter

Basking Shark

Norman MacCaig
b. 1911

To stub an oar on a rock where none should be,
To have it rise with a slounge out of sea,
Is a thing that happened once (too often) to me.

But not too often – though enough. I count as gain
That once I met, on a sea tin-tacked with rain,
That roomsized monster with a matchbox brain.

He displaced more than water. He shoggled me
Centuries back – this decadent townee
Shook on a wrong branch of his family tree.

Swish up the dirt and, when it settles, a spring
Is all the clearer. I saw me in one fling,
Emerging from the slime of everything.

So who's the monster? The thought made me grow pale
For twenty seconds while, sail after sail,
The tall fin slid away and then the tail.

Death of a Whale

John Blight
b. 1913

When the mouse died, there was a sort of pity:
The tiny, delicate creature made for grief.
Yesterday, instead, the dead whale on the reef
Drew an excited multitude to the jetty.
How must a whale die to wring a tear?
Lugubrious death of a whale; the big
Feast for the gulls and sharks; the tug
Of the tide simulating life still there,
Until the air, polluted, swings this way
Like a door ajar from a slaughterhouse.
Pooh! pooh! spare us, give us the death of a mouse
By its tiny hole; not this in our lovely bay.
– Sorry, we are, too, when a child dies;
But at the immolation of a race, who cries?

My normal dwelling is the lungs of swine,
  My normal shape a worm,
But other dwellings, other shapes, are mine
  Within my natural term.
Dimly I see my life, of all, the sign,
  Of better lives the germ.

The pig, though I am inoffensive, coughs,
  Finding me irritant:
My eggs go with the contents of the troughs
  From mouth to excrement –
The pig thus thinks, perhaps, he forever doffs
  His niggling resident.

The eggs lie unconsidered in the dung
  Upon the farmyard floor,
Far from the scarlet and sustaining lung:
  But happily a poor
And humble denizen provides a rung
  To make ascension sure.

The earthworm eats the eggs; inside the warm
  Cylinder larvae hatch:
For years, if necessary, in this form
  I wait the lucky match
That will return me to my cherished norm,
  My ugly pelt dispatch.

Strangely, it is the pig himself becomes
  The god inside the car:
His greed devours the earthworms; so the slums
  Of his intestines are
The setting for the act when clay succumbs
  And force steers for its star.

The larvae burrow through the bowel wall
  And, having to the dregs
Drained ignominy, gain the lung's great hall.
  They change. Once more, like pegs,
Lungworms are anchored to the rise and fall
  – And start to lay their eggs.

Roy Fuller
  b. 1912

Dolphin

What does this mean? The individual,
  Nature, mutation, strife?
I feel, though I am simple, still the whole
  Is complex; and that life –
A huge, doomed throbbing – has a wiry soul
  That must escape the knife.

When I went into my room, at mid-morning,
Say ten o'clock . . .
My room, a crash-box over that great stone rattle
The Via de'Bardi . . .

When I went into my room at mid-morning,
Why? . . . a bird!

A bird
Flying round the room in insane circles.

In insane circles!
. . . A bat!

A disgusting bat
At mid-morning! . . .

Out! Go out!

Round and round and round
With a twitchy, nervous, intolerable flight,
And a neurasthenic lunge,
And an impure frenzy;
A bat, big as a swallow.

Out, out of my room!

The venetian shutters I push wide
To the free, calm, upper air;
Loop back the curtains . . .

Man and Bat

D. H. Lawrence
1885–1930

Now out, out from my room!

So to drive him out, flickering with my white handkerchief: *Go!*
But he will not.

Round and round and round
In an impure haste,
Fumbling, a beast in air,
And stumbling, lunging and touching the walls, the bell-wires
About my room!

Always refusing to go out into the air
Above that crash-gulf of the Via de'Bardi,
Yet blind with frenzy, with cluttered fear.

At last he swerved into the window bay,
But blew back, as if an incoming wind blew him in again.
A strong inrushing wind.

And round and round and round!
Blundering more insane, and leaping, in throbs, to clutch at a corner,
At a wire, at a bell-rope:
On and on, watched relentless by me, round and round in my room,
Round and round and dithering with tiredness and haste and increasing
        delirium
Flicker-splashing round my room.

I would not let him rest;
Not one instant cleave, cling like a blot with his breast to the wall
In an obscure corner.
Not an instant!
I flicked him on,
Trying to drive him through the window.

Again he swerved into the window bay
And I ran forward, to frighten him forth.
But he rose, and from a terror worse than me he flew past me
Back into my room, and round, round, round in my room
Clutch, cleave, stagger,
Dropping about the air
Getting tired.

Something seemed to blow him back from the window
Every time he swerved at it;
Back on a strange parabola, then round, round, dizzy in my room.

He *could* not go out,
I also realised . . .
It was the light of day which he could not enter,
Anymore than I could enter the white-hot door of a blast-furnace.

He could not plunge into the daylight that streamed at the window.
It was asking too much of his nature.

Worse even than the hideous terror of me with my handkerchief
Saying: *Out, go out!* . . .
Was the horror of white daylight in the window!

So I switched on the electric light, thinking: *Now
The outside will seem brown* . . .
But no.
The outside did not seem brown,
And he did not mind the yellow electric light.

Silent!
He was having a silent rest.
But never!
Not in my room.

Round and round and round
Near the ceiling as if in a web,
Staggering;
Plunging, falling out of the web,
Broken in heaviness,
Lunging blindly,
Heavier;
And clutching, clutching for one second's pause,
Always, as if for one drop of rest,
One little drop.

And I!
Never, I say . . .
Go out!

Flying slower,
Seeming to stumble, to fall in air.
Blind-weary.

Yet never able to pass the whiteness of light into freedom . . .
A bird would have dashed through, come what might.

Fall, sink, lurch, and round and round
Flicker, flicker-heavy;
Even wings heavy:
And cleave in a high corner for a second, like a clot, also a prayer.

But no.
Out, you beast.

Then he fell in a corner, palpitating, spent.
And there, a clot, he squatted and looked at me.
With sticking-out, bead-berry eyes, black,
And improper derisive ears,
And shut wings,
And brown, furry body.

Brown, nut-brown, fine fur!
But it might as well have been hair on a spider; thing
With long, black-paper ears.

So, a dilemma!
He squatted there like something unclean.

No, he must not squat, nor hang, obscene, in my room

Yet nothing on earth will give him courage to pass the sweet fire of day.

What then?
Hit him and kill him and throw him away?

Nay,
I didn't create him.
Let the God that created him be responsible for his death. . . .
Only, in the bright day, I will not have this clot in my room.

Let the God who is maker of bats watch with them in their unclean
        corners . . .
I admit a God in every crevice,

But not bats in my room;
Nor the God of bats, while the sun shines.

So out, out, you brute! . . .
And he lunged, flight-heavy, away from me, sideways, *a sghembo!*
And round and round and round my room, a clot with wings,
Impure even in weariness.

Wings dark skinny and flapping the air,
Lost their flicker.
Spent.

He fell again with a little thud
Near the curtain on the floor.
And there lay.

Ah death, death
You are no solution!
Bats must be bats.

Only life has a way out.
And the human soul is fated to wide-eyed responsibility
In life.

So I picked him up in a flannel jacket,
Well covered, lest he should bite me.
For I would have had to kill him if he'd bitten me, the impure one . . .
And he hardly stirred in my hand, muffled up.

Hastily, I shook him out of the window
And away he went!
Fear craven in his tail.
Great haste, and straight, almost bird straight above the Via de'Bardi.
Above that crash-gulf of exploding whips,
Towards the Borgo San Jacopo.

And now, at evening, as he flickers over the river
Dipping with petty triumphant flight, and tittering over the sun's
    departure,
I believe he chirps, pipistrello, seeing me here on this terrace writing:
There he sits, the long loud one!
But I am greater than he . . .
I escaped him . . .

(Remember, I beseech thee, that thou has made me as the clay; and wilt thou bring me into dust again? – Job x. 9.)

The Beast His Brother

Francis
Quarles
(from
'Emblems',
Bk. III, No. 5)
1592–1644

Thus from the bosom of the new-made earth
Poor man was delved, and had his unknown birth;
The same the stuff, the self-same hand doth trim
The plant that fades, the beast that dies, and him:
One was their sire, one was their common mother,
Plants are his sisters, and the beast his brother,
The elder too; beasts draw the self-same breath,
Wax old alike, and die the self-same death:
Plants grow as he, with fairer robes array'd;
Alike they flourish, and alike they fade:
The beast in sense exceeds him, and, in growth,
The three-aged oak doth thrice exceed them both.
Why look'st thou then so big, thou little span
Of earth? what art thou more in being man?

Over to You

Evolution tells us that all living creatures are related, but man is set apart by his awareness of himself and of other creatures. The poems in OTHER KINGDOM register this awareness, showing man in relation to various members of the animal kingdom.

here's a little mouse Attempt a poem in the style of e. e. cummings about a caterpillar, a spider, a dragonfly, a tortoise or any other small creature.

The Jaguar (i) Imagine that the poet had made various thumbnail sketches of zoo creatures before selecting those included in the first two verses. Write one or two of these other items. (ii) What visions may pass through the jaguar's brain as he paces his cage?

Harassed Creatures Perhaps you have read *Animal Farm,* in which the animals revolt against their human master. With this idea in mind, imagine one of the animals here talking to his descendants about the condition of animals now and then. Some reference to 'factory farming' might help. Write the dialogue.

Cow Dance 'teats like bagpipes'; 'a milk-filled grenade'; 'harridans gone dancing'. Choose another animal and try to describe it in words as vivid or amusing as these.

Mouse, Dog, Jaguar, Cow Dance Get someone to play you the music by Saint-Saëns called *Carnival of the Animals.* Then suggest what sort of music might suit one or more of these four creatures. Some details in the poems might help you.

The Heron (i) Describe another part of the scene which emphasises by contrast the stillness of the heron, as he peers into the water. (ii) As dusk falls the heron flies away; the landscape takes on a different appearance. What does the bird see as he flies home over the darkening sea and land?

On a Goldfinch Starved to Death (i) In a dream the 'gentle swain' sees and hears the bird in eerie fashion. Follow the dream until the sleeper wakes. (ii) In the morning he finds the bird dead. What are his feelings and actions now?

The Windhover The poet finds the beauty, power and control of the kestrel as moving as those of Christ himself. Choose another wild creature and write about its seemingly human or divine qualities.

The Eagle and the Assembly of Animals (i) The last three lines of the poem suggest that humans, like the animals in the fable, are rarely content with themselves as they are. To illustrate this, imagine a group of four or five people complaining to a 'judge'. Conclude with an unexpected 'solution'. (ii) Try your hand at a fable (with animal characters) dealing with a human weakness (like hypocrisy, conceit, bribery or 'sitting on the fence').

In the Snake Park (i) Imagine that when the girl comes round she is in a rather feverish state of mind. Describe her recollection of the Snake Park incident as she speaks to the person looking after her. (ii) A playwright sees in the poem the seeds of a powerful drama. He jots down brief notes on plot and character. What might he have written?

Lizards and Snakes (i) Tell of an incident involving Aunt Martha and bats. (ii) Describe a creature which in certain circumstances could be taken for a monster of legend or fantasy.

In the Snake Park and *Lizards and Snakes* A writer reads these poems and decides to visit a herpetarium to have another look at snakes and lizards. He finds they have their attractive side after all. Write his account of two or three of the creatures.

The Fish Imagine you can follow the fish as it dives back into the deep. Describe the next few minutes or hours of its life.

Death of a Whale John Blight suggests that we do not feel the same about the deaths of different creatures. Choose two or three of the other creatures in the section and describe their death and how it might affect you.

Man and Bat Read some of Lawrence's other animal poems (for example *Snake, Mountain Lion, Kangaroo*) and write about an animal of your own choice. Bring in the sense of kinship with the animals.

– The section as a whole

(i) Are we sentimental about animals? Look at the poems again to help you decide.

(ii) Most of these poems show men looking at creatures. Write about a creature looking at a man.

(iii) Say which animal seems to you least promising as a subject for writing. (You might look again at Roy Fuller's poem about a lungworm.) Then write a poem or prose piece about it, remembering that it may have unsuspected elegance or fascination or power to teach us a lesson.

(iv) Look at pictures or film of one of the creatures in the poems and mention some other intriguing features the poet might have included.

(v) We often say animals don't feel or know much. Which animals in the section might seem to be exceptions to this?

(vi) Write a comic dialogue between a large and a small creature.

Further Reading *

Though we are related to the animals we tend to think of them as belonging to another kingdom, and many modern poets have tried to probe their mystery. Lawrence is one of the most perceptive. 'Snake', 'Humming Bird' (8) and 'Bat' (2) are well known, and in the *Collected Poems* (H) are also to be found 'Mosquito', 'Fish', 'Baby Tortoise', 'Tortoise Shell', 'Tortoise Family', 'Tortoise Gallantry', 'Tortoise Shout', 'Turkey Cock', 'Eagle in New Mexico', 'The Blue Jay', 'The Ass', 'He Goat', 'Elephant', 'Kangaroo', 'Mountain Lion' and 'The Red Wolf'. Ted Hughes is also fascinated by wild creatures, and 'Second Glance at a Jaguar' (in *Wodwo:* F) may be compared with his other jaguar poem. Some other animal poems of his are: 'Pike', 'View of a Pig' and 'Esther's Tomcat' (in 11); 'An Otter' (10); 'Hawk Roosting' (11, 12). 13 gives these and 'The Bull Moses' and 'Thrushes'. Cats galore are found in *Old Possum's Book of Practical Cats* (Eliot: F), to which may be added 'On a Favourite Cat' (Gray: Os); 'The Combat' (Muir: *Collected Poems:* F) and 'Cat' (Dunlop: 9). Other animals of various size are in 'To a Mouse' (Burns: 1); the rats in 'The Pied Piper' (Browning: 1); 'Hedgehog' (Thwaite: 9, 11); 'Epitaph on a Hare' (Cowper: Os); 'Sheepdog Trials in Hyde Park' (Day Lewis: 9); 'Hart-Leap Well' (Wordsworth: Os); 'The Zebras' (R. Campbell: 4, 8); 'The Donkey' (Chesterton: 1); 'Nicholas Nye' (De La Mare: 1); 'The Lamb' and 'The Tyger' (Blake: Os); 'Au Jardin des Plantes' (Wain: 13); 'The Bull' (Hodgson: *Collected Poems:* M). Water creatures are seen in 'The Pike' (Blunden: Poems: COL); 'Porpoises' (Walker: 13); 'The Birth of a Shark' (Wevill: 13); 'The Fish' (Brooke: Poems: SJ) and '*The Whale*' (Donne: 2) and birds in '*Owl*' (MacBeth: 13); 'At Porthcothan' (Middleton: 13); 'Death of a Bird' (Silkin: 5); 'The Wild Swans at Coole' (Yeats: 10, 12); 'The Swans' (Dyment: 11); 'Pigeons' (Kell: 9); 'Stork in Jersey', 'Town Owl' and 'Cock Pheasant' (Lee: 11) and 'To a Skylark' (Shelley: Os). Animals are compared with men, almost in Whitman's style, in 'The Animals' (Muir: 8) and 'Me and the Animals' (Holbrook: 13). A useful creature-by-creature anthology is *The Penguin Book of Animal Verse*.

If you enjoy short stories, the following, based on animal life, might appeal to you: Freeman: 'The Cat'; Bruce: 'Natuk'; Callaghan: 'Day of Grace'; and Lummins: 'The Bite of the Pichu Cuate' (in 16); 'The Wedge-Tailed Eagle' (Dutton) and 'The Rain Horse' (T. Hughes in 18); and 'The Conger Eel' (O'Flaherty) and 'The Blue Bead' (Burke in 19). A graphic account of 'Shooting an Elephant' is in *Selected Essays* (Orwell: P), while the same writer's *Animal Farm* (P) is a fable. The same technique in miniature is found in Aesop's *Fables* (P). Animals with semi-human characters are in Williamson's *Tarka the Otter* and *Salar the Salmon* (L) and Kipling's *Jungle Books* (M). Hosts of intriguing creatures are to be found in *My Family and Other Animals* (P), *The Drunken Forest*

* For explanation of symbols see p. 30.

(P) and *Encounters with Animals* (H) by Gerald Durrell. Longer accounts of man's dealings with single creatures are White: *The Goshawk* (CA, P, 15); Gallico: *The Snow Goose* (L); Farr: *Seal Morning* (HU); Maxwell: *Ring of Bright Water* (L, PA); Mankowitz: *A Kid for Two Farthings* (DE, Consul); Guillot: *Kpo the Leopard* (H); and Melville: *Moby Dick* (D). The last may be read in conjunction with *Of Whales and Men* (Robertson: PA) and *South Latitude* (Ommanney: L) while *North After Seals* (T. Williamson: L) also shows us animals in a remote setting. A different kind of pursuit is in *Zoo Quest for a Dragon* (Attenborough: PA). Two animal classics are *Call of the Wild* (London: L) and *Jock of the Bushveldt* (Fitzpatrick: L). For those unable to travel far, the *Romany* series (e.g. *A Romany in the Country*) (Evens: Epworth) may remind us of the interesting creatures to be found at home.

Animals make rather capricious *dramatis personae* (though Shakespeare found the need for a dog and a bear). *Androcles and the Lion* (Shaw: P) has some hilarious moments, and the animals in *Noah* (Obey: H) require brilliant acting. The Brothers Capek's *Life of the Insects* is a fable. The *May We Recommend* series (L) includes versions of *Alice in Wonderland* (Book 1) and *Moby Dick* (Book 6). Like *Alice, Toad of Toad Hall* and *The Reluctant Dragon* (FR), based on stories by K. Graham, seem to appeal to audiences of all ages. Another dragon play is Bolt's *The Thwarting of Baron Bolligrew* (FR), in which the manifestations of the species are limited to tails, eyes and roaring.

V New Men

The secret of those hills was stone, and cottages
Of that stone made,
And crumbling roads
That turned on sudden hidden villages.

Now over these small hills they have built the concrete
That trails black wire:
Pylons, those pillars
Bare like nude, giant girls that have no secret.

The valley with its gilt and evening look
And the green chestnut
Of customary root
Are mocked dry like the parched bed of a brook.

But far above and far as sight endures
Like whips of anger
With lightning's danger
There runs the quick perspective of the future.

This dwarfs our emerald country by its trek
So tall with prophecy:
Dreaming of cities
Where often clouds shall lean their swan-white neck.

Ah, you should see Cynddylan on a tractor.
Gone the old look that yoked him to the soil;
He's a new man now, part of the machine,
His nerves of metal and his blood oil.
The clutch curses, but the gears obey
His least bidding, and lo, he's away
Out of the farmyard, scattering hens.
Riding to work now as a great man should,
He is the knight at arms breaking the fields'
Mirror of silence, emptying the wood
Of foxes and squirrels and bright jays.

*The
Pylons*

*Stephen
Spender
b. 1909*

*Cynddylan
on a
Tractor*

*R. S. Thomas
b. 1913*

The sun comes over the tall trees
Kindling all the hedges, but not for him
Who runs his engine on a different fuel.
And all the birds are singing, bills wide in vain,
As Cynddylan passes proudly up the lane.

To a Loco-motive in Winter

Walt Whitman
1819–92

Thee for my recitative,
Thee in the driving storm even as now, the snow, the winter-day
    declining,
Thee in thy panoply, thy measur'd dual throbbing and thy beat con-
    vulsive,
Thy black cylindric body, golden brass and silvery steel,
Thy ponderous side-bars, parallel and connecting rods, gyrating,
    shuttling at thy sides,
Thy metrical, now swelling pant and roar, now tapering in the distance,
Thy great protruding head-light fix'd in front,
Thy long, pale, floating vapor-pennants, tinged with delicate purple,
The dense and murky clouds out-belching from thy smoke-stack,
Thy knitted frame, thy springs and valves, the tremulous twinkle of thy
    wheels,
Thy train of cars, behind, obedient, merrily following,
Through gale or calm, now swift, now slack, yet steadily careering ;
Type of the modern – emblem of motion and power – pulse of the
    continent,
For once come serve the Muse and merge in verse, even as here I see
    thee,
With storm and buffeting gusts of wind and falling snow,
By day thy warning ringing bell to sound its notes,
By night thy silent signal lamps to swing.

Fierce-throated beauty !
Roll through my chant with all thy lawless music, thy swinging lamps
    at night,
Thy madly-whistled laughter, echoing, rumbling like an earthquake,
    rousing all,
Law of thyself complete, thine own track firmly holding,
(No sweetness debonair of tearful harp or glib piano thine,)
Thy trills of shrieks by rocks and hills return'd,
Launch'd o'er the prairies wide, across the lakes,
To the free skies unpent and glad and strong.

Smoke from the train-gulf blunders upward, the brakes of cars
Pipe as the policeman pivoting round raises his flat hand, bars
With his figure of a monolith Pharaoh the queue of fidgety machines
(Chromium dogs on the bonnet, faces behind the triplex screens).
Behind him the streets run away between the proud glass of shops,
Cubical scent-bottles artificial legs arctic foxes and electric mops,
But beyond this centre the slumward vista thins like a diagram:
There, unvisited, are Vulcan's forges who doesn't care a tinker's damn.

Splayed outwards through the suburbs houses, houses for rest
Seducingly rigged by the builder, half-timbered houses with lips pressed
So tightly and eyes staring at the traffic through bleary haws
And only a six-inch gap of the racing earth in their concrete claws;
In these houses men as in a dream pursue the Platonic Forms
With wireless and cairn terriers and gadgets approximating to the fickle
    norms
And endeavour to find God and score one over the neighbour
By climbing tentatively upward on jerry-built beauty and sweated
    labour.

The lunch hour: the shops empty, shopgirls' faces relax
Diaphanous as green glass, empty as old almanacs
As incoherent with ticketed gewgaws tiered behind their heads
As the Burne-Jones windows in St Philip's broken by crawling leads;
Insipid colour, patches of emotion, Saturday thrills
(This theatre is sprayed with 'June') – the gutter take our old playbills,
Next week-end it is likely in the heart's funfair we shall pull
Strong enough on the handle to get back our money, or at any rate it
    is possible.

On shining lines the trams like vast sarcophagi move
Into the sky, plum after sunset, merging to duck's egg, barred with
    mauve
Zeppelin clouds, and Pentecost-like the cars' headlights bud
Out from sideroads and the traffic signals, crème-de-menthe or bull's
    blood,
Tell one to stop, the engine gently breathing, or to go on
To where like black pipes of organs in the frayed and fading zone
Of the West the factory chimneys on sullen sentry will all night wait
To call, in the harsh morning, sleep-stupid faces through the daily gate.

*Birming-
ham*

*Louis
MacNeice
1907–63*

Moon-man

The policeman stands on a plate of dirty light –
Statue of liberty, angel with flaming sword
As the whim takes him. His coat is white, not bright.

Screenwipers click and wheeze. Your sideways face
Wears its Etruscan look. How still we sit,
Staring from nowhere through two fans of space.

We, too, are in neutral. My one hand on the wheel
Has an underwater look, a growth look. I
Pick it from there to make it seem more real.

Completely other people come and go
In the completely other world. They'd speak
Black cubes and cones – some tongue we do not know.

The space between your shoulder and mine is full
Of space – you are ten million miles away . . .
The angel shuffles in his sleazy pool.

– We're off. You're back. Through fans of space I see
Comets and constellations and, glancing down,
A glove-black scorpion perched on one bright knee.

Traffic Stop

Norman
MacCaig
b. 1911

A man on his own in a car
    Is revenging himself on his wife;
He opens the throttle and bubbles with dottle
    And puffs at his pitiful life.

'She's losing her looks very fast,
    She loses her temper all day;
That lorry won't let me get past,
    This Mini is blocking my way.

'Why can't you step on it and shift her!
    I can't go on crawling like this!
At breakfast she said that she wished I was dead –
    Thank heaven we don't have to kiss.

*Meditation
on the
A30*

John Betjeman
b. 1906

'I'd like a nice blonde on my knee
    And one who won't argue or nag.
Who dares to come hooting at *me*?
    I only give way to a Jag.

'You're barmy or plastered, I'll pass you, you bastard –
    I will overtake you. I *will!*'
As he clenches his pipe, his moment is ripe
    And the corner's accepting its kill.

*

On the Move

*'Man you
gotta go'*

*Thom Gunn
b. 1929*

The blue jay scuffling in the bushes follows
Some hidden purpose, and the gust of birds
That spurts across the field, the wheeling swallows,
Have nested in the trees and undergrowth.
Seeking their instinct, or their poise, or both,
One moves with an uncertain violence
Under the dust thrown by a baffled sense
Or the dull thunder of approximate words.

On motorcycles, up the road, they come:
Small, black, as flies hanging in heat, the Boys,
Until the distance throws them forth, their hum
Bulges to thunder held by calf and thigh.
In goggles, donned impersonality,
In gleaming jackets trophied with the dust,
They strap in doubt – by hiding it, robust –
And almost hear a meaning in their noise.

Exact conclusion of their hardiness
Has no shape yet, but from known whereabouts
They ride, direction where the tires press.
They scare a flight of birds across the field:
Much that is natural, to the will must yield.
Men manufacture both machine and soul,
And use what they imperfectly control
To dare a future from the taken routes.

It is a part solution, after all.
One is not necessarily discord
On earth; or damned because, half animal,
One lacks direct instinct, because one wakes
Afloat on movement that divides and breaks.
One joins the movement in a valueless world,
Choosing it, till, both hurler and the hurled,
One moves as well, always toward, toward.

A minute holds them, who have come to go:
The self-defined, astride the created will
They burst away; the towns they travel through
Are home for neither bird nor holiness,
For birds and saints complete their purposes.
At worst, one is in motion; and at best,
Reaching no absolute, in which to rest,
One is always nearer by not keeping still.

The streets are noisy
with the movement of passing motors.
The coffee bars get fuller.
The leather-jacket groups begin to gather,
stand, and listen, pretending they are
looking for trouble.
The juke box plays its continuous
tune, music appreciated by Most.
The aroma of Espresso
coffee fills the nostrils and
the night.
Motorbikes pull up.
Riders dismount and join
their friends in the gang.
They stand, smoking, swearing,
playing with the girls;
making a teenage row.
They pretend not to notice the drizzle
falling out of the dark,
because you've got to be hard to
be a leather-jacket.

**Leather-Jackets,
Bikes and
Birds**

Robert Davies
b. 1946

A couple
in a corner, snogging,
hope the motor lights will not be
dipped too much,
so that the others will see them.
They must all have recognition;
there must always be enough
leather-jackets around them,
the same as theirs.
The street lamp on the side
of the street shows the rain
for what it is — wet and cold.
But it does not show their faces
for what they are.

Unholy Marriage

*Police are
seeking to
identify the
pillion rider
who was
also killed*

*David
Holbrook
b. 1923*

Her mother bore her, father cared
And clothed her body, young and neat.
The careful virgin had not shared
Cool soft anointment of her breast
Or any other sweet,
But kept herself for best.

How sweet she would have been in bed,
Her bridegroom sighing in her hair,
His tenderness heaped on her head,
Receiving benediction from her breast
With every other fair
She kept for him, the best.

Who she is now they do not know
Assembling her body on a sheet.
This foolish virgin shared a blow
That drove her almost through a stranger's breast
And all her sweet
Mingles with his in dust.

Unwilling marriage, her blood runs with one
Who bought for a few pounds and pence
A steel machine able to 'do a ton',
Not knowing at a ton a straw will pierce a breast:
No wheel has built-in sense,
Not yet the shiniest and best.

And so, 'doing a ton', in fog and night
Before he could think, Christ! or she could moan
There came a heavy tail without a light
And many tons compressed each back to breast
And blood and brain and bone
Mixed, lay undressed.

Anointed only by the punctured oil
Poured like unleashed wind or fire from bag
Sold by some damned magician out to spoil
The life that girded in this young girl's breast
Now never to unfurl her flag
And march love's happy quest.

Her mother hears the clock; her father sighs,
Takes off his boots: she's late tonight.
I hope she's a careful virgin: men have eyes
For cherished daughters growing in the breast.
Some news? They hear the gate –
A man comes: not the best.

Two minutes long it pitches through some bar:
Unreeling from a corner box, the sigh
Of this one, in his gangling finery
And crawling sideburns, wielding a guitar.

The limitations where he found success
Are ground on which he, panting, stretches out
In turn, promiscuously, by every note.
Our idiosyncrasy and our likeness.

Elvis Presley

Thom Gunn
b. 1929

Computers

We keep ourselves in touch with a mere dime:
Distorting hackneyed words in hackneyed songs
He turns revolt into a style, prolongs
The impulse to a habit of the time.

Whether he poses or is real, no cat
Bothers to say: the pose held is a stance,
Which, generation of the very chance
It wars on, may be posture for combat.

Red and green neon lights, the jazz hysteria,
for all-night movie and all-night cafeteria;
you feed all night in one, and sleep in the other,
and dream that a strip-tease queen was your sweetheart's mother.

A nickel for a coffee – half a dime for a seat;
the blondes and the guns are streamlined and complete;
streamlined, dreamlined, with wide open cactus spaces
between the four-foot teeth in the ten-foot faces.

Hot trumpets and hot trombones for a soft-sole shuffle!
Sailors, bring in your tattoos, park your duffel!
There's a green-tailed blue-eyed mermaid stinging my shoulder,
and I've got to pass out before I'm a minute older.

Sawdust, spittoon, no smoking, please excuse –
afloat or ashore we mind our p's and q's.
Longhorn stand back, shorthorn stand close, is all
the circular eye makes out on the circular wall.

And still the red neon lights go round and round,
the red mouth opens and drinks with never a sound, –
red on the Square, red on the jingling Palace,
where all night long you rumbaed and drank with Alice –

red on the tattoo artist's sign, that shakes
anchors and flags together, ships and snakes,
roses, and a pink Venus, on a shell,
la, la, all dancing feet in a neon hell –

*Nuit
Blanche:
North
End*

Conrad Aiken
b. 1889

while round and around the red beads wink, and faster
empty and open, pour and fill, disaster:
the red mouth opens and drinks, opens and winks,
drinks down the hotel wall, the drugstore, drinks

the Square, the statue, the bright red roofs of cabs,
and the cleaning-women, who arise with pails and swabs:
then stains the dawn, who, over the subway station,
steals in, the Sandals gray, but no elation.

Inexpensive Progress

John Betjeman
b. 1906

Encase your legs in nylons,
Bestride your hills with pylons
   O age without a soul;
Away with gentle willows
And all the elmy billows
   That through your valleys roll.

Let's say good-bye to hedges
And roads with grassy edges
   And winding country lanes;
Let all things travel faster
Where motor-car is master
   Till only Speed remains.

Destroy the ancient inn-signs
But strew the roads with tin signs
   'Keep Left', 'M4', 'Keep Out!'
Command, instruction, warning,
Repetitive adorning
   The rockeried roundabout;

For every raw obscenity
Must have its small 'amenity',
   Its patch of shaven green,
And hoardings look a wonder
In banks of floribunda
   With floodlights in between.

Leave no old village standing
Which could provide a landing
    For aeroplanes to roar,
But spare such cheap defacements
As huts with shattered casements
    Unlived-in since the war.

Let no provincial High Street
Which might be your or my street
    Look as it used to do,
But let the chain stores place here
Their miles of black glass facia
    And traffic thunder through.

And if there is some scenery,
Some unpretentious greenery,
    Surviving anywhere,
It does not need protecting
For soon we'll be erecting
    A Power Station there.

When all our roads are lighted
By concrete monsters sited
    Like gallows overhead,
Bathed in the yellow vomit
Each monster belches from it,
    We'll know that we are dead.

A newspaper is a collection of half-injustices
Which, bawled by boys from mile to mile,
Spreads its curious opinion
To a million merciful and sneering men,
While families cuddle the joys of the fireside
When spurred by tale of dire lone agony.
A newspaper is a court
Where every one is kindly and unfairly tried
By a squalor of honest men.
A newspaper is a market
Where wisdom sells its freedom
And melons are crowned by the crowd.

A Newspaper

Stephen Crane
1871–1900

A newspaper is a game
Where his error scores the player victory
While another's skill wins death.
A newspaper is a symbol;
It is feckless life's chronicle,
A collection of loud tales
Concentrating eternal stupidities,
That in remote ages lived unhaltered,
Roaming through a fenceless world.

An International Football Match

*Edmund
Blunden
b. 1896*

Some time the English name in sport was good,
The rigour of the game was the clear way.
The other player, it was understood,
Was as yourself, however went the day.
No poisoned mood lurked then for chance to strike.
From generous greatheart sprang the invitation
To meet in sunny hour and strive alike
And settle friendly odds in recreation.

Look where that shining name begins to fade.
Hear how, before the sport we preached and blessed
Is planned anew, each snarling retrograde
Prepares his malice for the coming guest.
Men cannot shoot a goal or jump a hurdle
Without a psychologic gas attack.
Strange that the milk of kindness here should curdle,
And English hands maul one white record black.

Ex-Basketball Player

John Updike
b. 1932

Pearl Avenue runs past the high-school lot,
Bends with the trolley tracks, and stops, cut off
Before it has a chance to go two blocks,
At Colonel McComsky Plaza. Berth's Garage
Is on the corner facing west, and there,
Most days, you'll find Flick Webb, who helps Berth out.

Flick stands tall among the idiot pumps —
Five on a side, the old bubble-head style,
Their rubber elbows hanging loose and low.
One's nostrils are two S's, and his eyes
An E and O. And one is squat, without
A head at all — more of a football type.

Once Flick played for the high-school team, the Wizards.
He was good: in fact, the best. In '46
He bucketed three hundred ninety points,
A county record still. The ball loved Flick.
I saw him rack up thirty-eight or forty
In one home game. His hands were like wild birds.

He never learned a trade, he just sells gas,
Checks oil, and changes flats. Once in a while,
As a gag, he dribbles an inner tube,
But most of us remember anyway.
His hands are fine and nervous on the lug wrench.
It makes no difference to the lug wrench, though.

Off work, he hangs around Mae's luncheonette.
Grease-gray and kind of coiled, he plays pinball,
Smokes those thin cigars, nurses lemon phosphates.
Flick seldom says a word to Mae, just nods
Beyond her face toward bright applauding tiers
Of Necco Wafers, Nibs, and Juju Beads.

The Scientists

Edmund
Blunden
b. 1896

How shall this thing be done?
How shall we make the lawless lightning run
In tracks compelled by us, its flame
Obedient grown to us and tame
As water played from marble Triton's gorge?
What change should seize this passionate fire
And keep him here at our desire,
The courier of our will, the servant of our forge?

Curious and maybe more
If we might gaze with an intenser eye
Into this star which burns and seems to try
To give us its strange lore.
There is the challenge, here are we aware
Of something in the air;
And only one thing needed, but that one
May seem faint dream. How shall this thing be done?

'I'll put a girdle round about the world
In forty seconds.' If you mean a chain
Of thought and news and sense, do not refrain;
But fancy oiled and curled
Has entertained before. In earnest then,
You mean to traverse weather fair or foul,
Speak, sing, play Shakespeare through the hemispheres,
Serene through distance and through tempest's howl –
Bear London's voice to Tokyo? Gentlemen,
I will subscribe when your machine appears.

Professor, one small doubt –
Here is a body, which this morning smiled
A beautiful and energetic child.
What is this wave of life, and whence welled out?
Why, how so sharply vanished? Will not you,
Having accomplished such a host of things
Which I repeated x times could not do,
Come at this other secret? Find the nerve,
Discern the essential curve,
And build the new power-station, the reserve?
You know that easy dust which makes a gun
Immensely active –
$\qquad$ 'This too shall be done.'

ee fall

Mental Cases

Wilfred Owen
1893–1918

Who are these? Why sit they here in twilight?
Wherefore rock they, purgatorial shadows,
Drooping tongues from jaws that slob their relish,
Baring teeth that leer like skulls' teeth wicked?
Stroke on stroke of pain, – but what slow panic,
Gouged these chasms round their fretted sockets?
Ever from their hair and through their hands' palms
Misery swelters. Surely we have perished
Sleeping, and walk hell; but who these hellish?

– These are men whose minds the Dead have ravished.
Memory fingers in their hair of murders,
Multitudinous murders they once witnessed.
Wading sloughs of flesh these helpless wander,
Treading blood from lungs that had loved laughter.
Always they must see these things and hear them,
Batter of guns and shatter of flying muscles,
Carnage incomparable, and human squander,
Rucked too thick for these men's extrication.

Therefore still their eyeballs shrink tormented
Back into their brains, because on their sense
Sunlight seems a blood-smear; night comes blood-black;
Dawn breaks open like a wound that bleeds afresh
– Thus their heads wear this hilarious, hideous,
Awful falseness of set-smiling corpses.
– Thus their hands are plucking at each other;
Picking at the rope-knouts of their scourging;
Snatching after us who smote them, brother,
Pawing us who dealt them war and madness.

Walking Wounded

Vernon Scannell
b. 1922

A mammoth morning moved grey flanks and groaned
In the rusty hedges pale rags of mist hung;
The gruel of mud and leaves in the mauled lane
Smelled sweet, like blood. Birds had died or flown,
Their green and silent attics sprouting now
With branches of leafed steel, hiding round eyes
And ripe grenades ready to drop and burst.
In the ditch at the cross-roads the fallen rider lay

Hugging his dead machine and did not stir
At crunch of mortar, tantrum of a Bren
Answering a Spandau's manic jabber.
Then into sight the ambulances came,
Stumbling and churning past the broken farm,
The amputated sign-post and smashed trees,
Slow wagonloads of bandaged cries, square trucks
That rolled on ominous wheels, vehicles
Made mythopoeic by their mortal freight
And crimson crosses on the dirty white.
This grave procession passed, though, for a while,
The grinding of their engines could be heard,
A dark noise on the pallor of the morning,
Dark as dried blood; and then it faded, died.
The road was empty, but it seemed to wait –
Like a stage which knows the cast is in the wings –
Wait for a different traffic to appear.
The mist still hung in snags from dripping thorns;
Absent-minded guns still sighed and thumped.
And then they came, the walking wounded,
Straggling the road like convicts loosely chained,
Dragging at ankles exhaustion and despair.
Their heads were weighted down by last night's lead,
And eyes still drank the dark. They trailed the night
Along the morning road. Some limped on sticks;
Others wore rough dressings, splints and slings;
A few had turbanned heads, the dirty cloth
Brown-badged with blood. A humble brotherhood,
Not one was suffering from a lethal hurt,
They were not magnified by noble wounds,
There was no splendour in that company.
And yet, remembering after eighteen years,
In the heart's throat a sour sadness stirs;
Imagination pauses and returns
To see them walking still, but multiplied
In thousands now. And when heroic corpses
Turn slowly in their decorated sleep
And every ambulance has disappeared
The walking wounded still trudge down that lane,
And when recalled they must bear arms again.

Still falls the Rain –
Dark as the world of man, black as our loss –
Blind as the nineteen hundred and forty nails
Upon the Cross.

Still falls the Rain
With a sound like the pulse of the heart that is changed to the hammer-
      beat
In the Potter's Field, and the sound of the impious feet

On the Tomb:
            Still falls the Rain
In the Field of Blood where the small hopes breed and the human brain
Nurtures its greed, that worm with the brow of Cain.

Still falls the Rain
At the feet of the Starved Man hung upon the Cross.
Christ that each day, each night, nails there, have mercy on us –
On Dives and on Lazarus:
Under the Rain the sore and the gold are as one.

Still falls the Rain –
Still falls the Blood from the Starved Man's wounded Side:
He bears in His Heart all wounds, – those of the light that died,
The last faint spark
In the self-murdered heart, the wounds of the sad uncomprehending
      dark,
The wounds of the baited bear, –
The blind and weeping bear whom the keepers beat
On his helpless flesh . . . the tears of the hunted hare.

Still falls the Rain –
Then – O Ile leape up to my God: who pulles me doune –
See, see where Christ's blood streames in the firmament:
It flows from the Brow we nailed upon the tree
Deep to the dying, to the thirsting heart
That holds the fires of the world, – dark-smirched with pain
As Caesar's laurel crown.

Then sounds the voice of One who like the heart of man
Was once a child who among beasts has lain –
'Still do I love, still shed my innocent light, my Blood, for thee.'

dio telescope

***Still
Falls
the
Rain***

*The Raids,
1940.
Night and
Dawn*

*Edith Sitwell
1887–1964*

Over to You

Human nature does not change very much from age to age, though the people of every epoch seem to think there has never been another one like it. At the present time they are probably right, since the last few decades have seen some startling changes in man's environment. NEW MEN charts the poet's response to a few of these.

The Pylons   A helicopter follows the line of the pylons across country. Eventually they lead to an industrial area. Describe what the pilot sees, in particular the way in which man-made and natural objects mingle.

To a Locomotive in Winter   Did you feel the exhilaration of the poem? In something of the same manner describe the locomotive (i) going through a tunnel; (ii) passing over a large viaduct; (iii) grinding to a stop in a busy town station.

Cynddylan on a Tractor; To a Locomotive in Winter   Imagine that the two machines in these poems are in a museum of the future. People are examining them in fascination and amusement. Give some of their remarks.

Birmingham   (i) The poet's critical eye takes a further sweep round the city scene. What other things does he notice? (ii) Sketch a futuristic city background as a setting for the descendants of the people in the poem. Are their ideals and attitudes different from their ancestors'? (You might care to think of these people of the future at work, at home, at leisure, moving about, etc.)

Traffic Stop   (i) Note the striking description of the policeman in the first verse, and give a few other details of the street scene as the poet might see them. (ii) The driver of the car feels isolated from the people outside. Imagine yourself to be one of these and give your (perhaps hostile) thoughts as you observe those in the car.

Meditation on the A30   (i) A woman driver in an expensive car pulls out abruptly in front of this man. Give his thoughts (or words). (ii) As he rounds his last corner a chain of images flashes through his mind. Give a graphic account of these.

Leather-Jackets, Bikes and Birds   (i) Describe in more detail those involved in the 'teenage row' and the row itself. (ii) Give the comments of a few of these coffee-bar teenagers on the idea that they

> 'must have recognition;
> there must always be enough
> leather-jackets around them,
> the same as theirs.'

The notion of 'toughness' and following a fashion might be relevant.

On the Move; Leather-Jackets, Bikes and Birds; Unholy Marriage These three poems are concerned in different ways with motor-cycles and their riders. In any form of words you think suitable (chorus, contrasting voices, dialogue, echo, song, noise-words, etc.) explore the same theme from various angles, for example: power, menace, movement, playing a part, speed, parents, sex, noise – and many others.

Elvis Presley (i) Invent a suitable lyric for Elvis to sing. It might include an element of 'revolt'. (ii) If 'some cat' did in fact ask Elvis whether his singing was a pose, what reply might he make?

Nuit Blanche: North End Did you enjoy the racy style of this poem ('striptease queens'; 'streamlined, dreamlined'; 'park your duffel') and the change of mood at the end? Use some vivid or slangy expressions to describe a wild evening which ends with a complete contrast.

Inexpensive Progress Mr Betjeman often appears on television. Imagine he is questioned by an aggressive (and 'progressive') interviewer about some of the items in the poem. Give the questions and Mr Betjeman's replies.

An International Football Match (i) Describe two footballers in action: (i) a centre-forward in the 'good days' of sport prevented by tough opposition from scoring in the final seconds of the game; (ii) an inside forward of today indulging in a 'malicious' manoeuvre as he attempts to score. (iii) Do you agree with Blunden's complaint (made about thirty years ago) that the 'shining name' of sport is fading?

Ex-Basketball Player Sketch an hour or so in Flick's life as his memories of the football field merge with his work around the petrol station.

The Scientists If a dead child *were* brought to life, the press, radio and television would be full of strident and conflicting voices. Write items from two of these media, giving different views on the 'resurrection'. It might help if you recall some of the public disagreement about heart transplants, etc.

Mental Cases Imagine that Wilfred Owen, who fought in the First World War and was killed shortly before the Armistice, has returned to life. He is questioned by a young anti-war person about this poem and his own experiences. Give some of the dialogue. If you can enlist the help of someone who fought in the last war, you might try a tape-recording on the same lines.

Walking Wounded (i) You are one of the men in the ambulances. Describe your wounds and how you got them and your feelings as you see your companions and the shattered countryside all around. (ii) One of the walking wounded has rather different feelings. Give his point of view first as he trudges along and then later as he convalesces in hospital.

Mental Cases; Walking Wounded; Strange Meeting (Section II)   Taking these poems – which show the mental and physical suffering caused by modern war – as starting points, plan a composite tape-recording on the theme 'War in Our Era' – using whatever title you think best. Consider the use of extracts from these or other poems, protest songs, arguments, obituary notices, press reports on Vietnam and Nigeria, etc.

– *The section as a whole*

(i) Many of these poems criticise modern life. Which criticisms are the most serious?

(ii) A man from the distant past comes to life and encounters some of the people and machines in the poems. What might he say, think or do?

(iii) Write a letter to one of the poets in this section requesting him to write a poem about something technical or scientific. Explain why you would like to read such a poem, referring if you wish to the poet's own work.

(iv) Write a story about a being from space who arrives on earth in search of scientific information.

(v) Write a poem in the style of Betjeman about transistor radios or discothèques, or in the style of Whitman about an ocean liner or racing car.

(vi) A future historian, writing about 'The Civilization of the Twentieth Century', unearths this anthology and reads through this section. Certain poems set him thinking about the term 'civilization'. Write the notes he makes on them.

Further Reading *

This section surveys some features of modern life, especially those brought about by advances in technology. Michael Baldwin's poem 'Death on a Live Wire' (9) would give you another view of Spender's 'Pylons'. Machines have brought speed and mobility (and sometimes tragedy) as illustrated in 'Casey Jones' (2) and Spender's 'The Express' (1, 3). A motor-cycle crash is the subject of 'At Any Rate' (Michie: 9). 'Black Jackets' (Gunn: 13) probes the character of these young people, and may be compared with Webster's 'Street Gang' (9). Kirkup's 'Tea in a Space Ship' and 'No More Hiroshimas' give opposing views of technical progress (11). War figures largely in modern verse, and differing aspects of it are found in 'Children's Crusade 1939' (Brecht: 6); 'Death of an Aircraft' (Causley: 6, 11); 'Six Young Men (T. Hughes: 11) and 'Your Attention Please' (a nuclear attack) by P. Porter (9). The poems of Wilfred Owen, e.g. 'Spring Offensive', 'Greater Love' (10), 'Anthem for Doomed Youth' (8) and 'Exposure' (10, 12), remain some of the most compelling of the First World War. The general condition of modern man is the subject of 'The Unknown Citizen' (Auden: 10) and in lighter vein much of Betjeman, e.g. 'The Village Inn' (11) and 'Harvest Hymn' (in *High and Low*: MU). H. D. Carberry provides an 'Epitaph' on the age in 12.

A satirical view of much of modern life is offered by E. Waugh, e.g. in *The Loved One, Men at Arms, Put Out More Flags* and *Scoop* (P). Other shrewd observers are Muriel Spark in *The Go-Away Bird* (stories: P) and, going back a little, Fitzgerald in *The Diamond as Big as the Ritz and Other Stories* and *The Great Gatsby* (F). Hemingway's stories, e.g. *Men Without Women* (P), offer a more realistic account of our age. The same author's *For Whom The Bell Tolls* (P) deals with the Spanish Civil War, and fighting in different times and places may be shown in extracts from Graves: *Goodbye to All That* (P); Heller: *Catch 22* (COR); Mailer: *The Naked and the Dead* (Panther); and M. McCarthy: *Vietnam* (P). Classic escape stories are *Rogue Male* (Household: P) and *The Wooden Horse* (Williams: COL, 15). Some interesting comparisons may be made between the social conditions as depicted in Orwell's *Down and Out in Paris and London* and *The Road to Wigan Pier* (P), Bill Naughton's *A Roof Over Your Head* (B) and Wells' *Tono-Bungay* (L), and more recent pictures such as those sketched by Monica Dickens in *One Pair of Feet*, etc. (P), or more thoroughly by Braine in *Room at the Top* and *Life at the Top* (P) or Sillitoe in *Saturday Night and Sunday Morning* (PA). A possible future is described in *Nineteen Eighty-Four* (Orwell: P). Russell asks *Has Man a Future?* (P). A field much in the news recently is medicine, which the following Pan titles explore: Thorwald: *The Century of the Surgeon*; Sava: *Strange Cases*; Engel: *The Operation*; and Sargant: *Battle for the Mind*. With the last may be compared Packard's *The Hidden Persuaders* (P, 15). The following could provide useful

* For explanation of symbols see p. 30.

extracts on present-day problems: Galbraith: *The Affluent Society*; Larner and Tefferteller: *The Addict in the Street*; Jones: *Crime in a Changing Society*; Hoggart: *The Uses of Literacy* (15) (all P). R. Carson's *Silent Spring* (P) calls in question some of our scientific wisdom.

A group of plays dealing with contemporary problems is in *Worth a Hearing* (ed. Bradley: B). The same publishers also offer Wesker's *Chips with Everything*, dealing with the tensions in service life. War forms the background of *Incident at Vichy* by Miller (in *New American Drama*: P) and the other plays in the volume offer criticisms of modern life. G. Cooper's *Mathry Beacon* also has a war setting, while Shaw discusses the ethics of war in *Major Barbara* (P). O'Casey gives the Irish revolutionary background in *The Shadow of a Gunman, Juno and the Paycock* and *The Plough and the Stars* (D). Dilemmas arising from war are explored in *Marching Song* (J. Whiting in *Three Plays*: H), *The Long and the Short and the Tall* (W. Hall: H, P) and *Sergeant Musgrave's Dance* (Arden: ME). Violence or menace is seen in *Lee Harvey Oswald* (M. Hastings: P) and *The Birthday Party* (Pinter: ME). The problems of young people are explored in *A Taste of Honey* (S. Delaney: ME) and *Trilogy* – three plays by Wesker (P) covering the years 1936–59.

VI Dreams and Visions

When my mother died I was very young,
And my father sold me while yet my tongue
Could scarcely cry ' 'weep! 'weep! 'weep! 'weep!'
So your chimneys I sweep, and in soot I sleep.

There's little Tom Dacre, who cried when his head,
That curled like a lamb's back, was shaved: so I said
'Hush, Tom! never mind it, for when your head's bare
You know that the soot cannot spoil your white hair.'

And so he was quiet, and that very night,
As Tom was a-sleeping, he had such a sight! –
That thousands of sweepers, Dick, Joe, Ned, and Jack,
Were all of them locked up in coffins of black.

And by came an Angel who had a bright key,
And he opened the coffins and set all of them free;
Then down a green plain leaping, laughing, they run,
And wash in a river, and shine in the sun.

Then naked and white, all their bags left behind,
They rise upon clouds and sport in the wind;
And the angel told Tom, if he'd be a good boy,
He'd have God for his father, and never want joy.

And so Tom awoke; and we rose in the dark,
And got with our bags and our brushes to work.
Though the morning was cold, Tom was happy and warm;
So if all do their duty they need not fear harm.

The
Chimney
Sweep

William Blake
1757–1827

little tree

e. e. cummings
1894–1962

little tree
little silent Christmas tree
you are so little
you are more like a flower

who found you in the green forest
and were you very sorry to come away?
see   i will comfort you
because you smell so sweetly

i will kiss your cool bark
and hug you safe and tight
just as your mother would,
only don't be afraid

look   the spangles
that sleep all the year in a dark box
dreaming of being taken out and allowed to shine,
the balls the chains red and gold the fluffy threads,

put up your little arms
and i'll give them all to you to hold
every finger shall have its ring
and there won't be a single place dark or unhappy

then when you're quite dressed
you'll stand in the window for everyone to see
and how they'll stare!
oh but you'll be very proud

and my little sister and i will take hands
and looking up at our beautiful tree
we'll dance and sing
'Noel Noel'

146

My mother bore me in the southern wild,
And I am black, but O! my soul is white;
White as an angel is the English child,
But I am black, as if bereav'd of light.

My mother taught me underneath a tree,
And, sitting down before the heat of day,
She took me on her lap and kissèd me,
And, pointing to the east, began to say:

'Look on the rising sun, – there God does live,
And gives His light, and gives His heat away;
And flowers and trees and beasts and men receive
Comfort in morning, joy in the noonday.

'And we are put on earth a little space,
That we may learn to bear the beams of love;
And these black bodies and this sunburnt face
Is but a cloud, and like a shady grove.

'For when our souls have learn'd the heat to bear,
The cloud will vanish; we shall hear His voice,
Saying: "Come out from the grove, My love and care,
And round My golden tent like lambs rejoice." '

Thus did my mother say. and kissèd me;
And thus I say to little English boy.
When I from black and he from white cloud free,
And round the tent of God like lambs we joy,

I'll shade him from the heat, till he can bear
To lean in joy upon our Father's knee;
And then I'll stand and stroke his silver hair,
And be like him, and he will then love me.

The
Little
Black
Boy

William Blake
1757–1827

147

Fern Hill

Dylan Thomas
1914–53

Now as I was young and easy under the apple boughs
About the lilting house and happy as the grass was green,
   The night above the dingle starry,
      Time let me hail and climb
   Golden in the heydays of his eyes,
And honoured among wagons I was prince of the apple towns
And once below a time I lordly had the trees and leaves
      Trail with daisies and barley
   Down the rivers of the windfall light.

And as I was green and carefree, famous among the barns
About the happy yard and singing as the farm was home,
   In the sun that is young once only,
      Time let me play and be
   Golden in the mercy of his means,
And green and golden I was huntsman and herdsman, the calves
Sang to my horn, the foxes on the hills barked clear and cold,
      And the sabbath rang slowly
   In the pebbles of the holy streams.

All the sun long it was running, it was lovely, the hay
Fields high as the house, the tunes from the chimneys, it was air
   And playing, lovely and watery
      And fire green as grass.
   And nightly under the simple stars
As I rode to sleep the owls were bearing the farm away,
All the moon long I heard, blessed among stables, the nightjars
   Flying with the ricks, and the horses
      Flashing into the dark.

And then to awake, and the farm, like a wanderer white
With the dew, come back, the cock on his shoulder: it was all
   Shining, it was Adam and maiden,
      The sky gathered again
   And the sun grew round that very day.
So it must have been after the birth of the simple light
In the first, spinning place, the spellbound horses walking warm
   Out of the whinnying green stable
      On to the fields of praise.

And honoured among foxes and pheasants by the gay house
Under the new made clouds and happy as the heart was long,
   In the sun born over and over,
     I ran my heedless ways,
   My wishes ran through the house high hay
And nothing I cared, at my sky blue trades, that time allows
In all his tuneful turning so few and such morning songs
   Before the children green and golden
     Follow him out of grace,

Nothing I cared, in the lamb white days, that time would take me
Up to the swallow thronged loft by the shadow of my hand,
   In the moon that is always rising,
     Nor that riding to sleep
   I should hear him fly with the high fields
And wake to the farm forever fled from the childless land.
Oh as I was young and easy in the mercy of his means,
    Time held me green and dying
   Though I sang in my chains like the sea.

My long two-pointed ladder's sticking through a tree
Toward heaven still,
And there's a barrel that I didn't fill
Beside it, and there may be two or three
Apples I didn't pick upon some bough,
But I am done with apple-picking now.
Essence of winter sleep is on the night,
The scent of apples: I am drowsing off.
I cannot rub the strangeness from my sight
I got from looking through a pane of glass
I skimmed this morning from the drinking trough
And held against the world of hoary grass.
It melted, and I let it fall and break.
But I was well
Upon my way to sleep before it fell,
And I could tell
What form my dreaming was about to take.

After Apple-picking

Robert Frost
1874–1963

Pyrotechnics

Magnified apples appear and disappear,
Stem end and blossom end,
And every fleck of russet showing clear.
My instep arch not only keeps the ache,
It keeps the pressure of a ladder-round.
I feel the ladders sway as the boughs bend.
And I keep hearing from the cellar bin
The rumbling sound
Of load on load of apples coming in.
For I have had too much
Of apple-picking: I am overtired
Of the great harvest I myself desired.
There were ten thousand fruit to touch,
Cherish in hand, lift down, and not let fall.
For all
That struck the earth,
No matter if not bruised or spiked with stubble,
Went surely to the cider-apple heap
As of no worth.
One can see what will trouble
This sleep of mine, whatever sleep it is.
Were he not gone,
The woodchuck could say whether it's like his
Long sleep, as I describe its coming on,
Or just some human sleep.

De Lord he thought he'd make a man —
Dese bones gwine to rise again;
Made him out-a dirt an' a little bit o' sand —
Dese bones gwine to rise again.

Refrain
I know it, 'deed I know it,
Dese bones gwine to rise again.

Adam was de fust he made —
He put him on de bank and lay him in de shade —

Dese Bones Gwine To Rise Again

Anonymous

Thought he'd make a 'ooman, too, –
Didn't know 'xactly what to do –

Took a rib from Adam's side –
Made Miss Eve for to be his bride –

Put 'em in a gyarden, rich and fair –
Tol' em dey might eat whatever wuz dere –

But to one tree dey mus' not go –
Mus' leave de apples dere to grow –

Ol' Miss Eve come walkin' round –
Spied a tree all loaded down –

Sarpint quoiled around a chunk –
At Miss Eve his eye he wunk –

Firs' she took a little pull –
Den she fill her apron full –

Den Adam took a little slice –
Smack his lips an' say 'twas nice –

De Lord he come a-wanderin' roun' –
Spied dem peelin's on de groun' –

De Lord he speaks wid a monstrus voice –
Shuck dis ol' worl' to its ve'y joists –

'Adam, Adam, where art thou?'
'Heah, Marse Lord, Ise a-comin' now.'

'Stole my apples, I believe?'
'No, Marse Lord, but I spec' it wuz Eve.'

De Lord he riz up in his wrath –
Told 'em, 'Yo' beat it down de path.'

'Out o' dis gyarden you mus' git.
Earn yo' living by yo' sweat.'

He put an angel at de do' –
Tol' 'em not to never come dere no mo' –

Ob dis tale dere ain' no mo' –
Dese bones gwine to rise again.
Eve eat de apple, gib Adam de co' –
Dese bones gwine to rise again.

I know it, 'deed I know it,
Dese bones gwine to rise again.

I know some lonely houses off the road
A robber'd like the look of, –
Wooden barred,
And windows hanging low,
Inviting to a portico,

Where two could creep:
One hand the tools,
The other peep
To make sure all's asleep.
Old-fashioned eyes,
Not easy to surprise!

How orderly the kitchen'd look by night,
With just a clock, –
But they could gag the tick,
And mice won't bark;
And so the walls don't tell,
None will.

A pair of spectacles ajar just stir –
An almanac's aware.
Was it the mat winked,
Or a nervous star?
The moon slides down the stair
To see who's there.

There's plunder, – where?
Tankard, or spoon,
Earring, or stone,
A watch, some ancient brooch
To match the grandmamma,
Staid sleeping there.

I Know Some Lonely Houses

Emily
Dickinson
1830–86

Aurora Borealis

Day rattles, too,
Stealth's slow;
The sun has got as far
As the third sycamore.
Screams chanticleer,
'Who's there?'

And echoes, trains away,
Sneer – 'Where?'
While the old couple, just astir,
Think that the sunrise left the door ajar!

A captain bold, in Halifax, who dwelt in country quarters,
Seduced a maid, who hang'd herself, one morning, in her garters,
His wicked conscience smited him, he lost his stomach daily,
He took to drinking ratafee, and thought upon Miss Bailey.
Oh, Miss Bailey! unfortunate Miss Bailey.

One night betimes he went to rest, for he had caught a fever,
Says he, 'I am a handsome man, but I'm a gay deceiver;'
His candle just at twelve o'clock began to burn quite palely,
A ghost stepped up to his bedside, and said, 'Behold Miss Bailey.'
Oh, Miss Bailey! unfortunate Miss Bailey.

'Avaunt, Miss Bailey,' then he cried, 'your face looks white and mealy,'
'Dear Captain Smith,' the ghost replied, 'you've used me ungenteelly;
The Crowner's Quest goes hard with me, because I've acted fraily,
And parson Biggs won't bury me, though I am dead Miss Bailey.'
Oh, Miss Bailey! unfortunate Miss Bailey.

'Dear Corpse,' said he, 'since you and I accounts must once for all close,
I've really got a one pound note in my regimental small clothes;
'Twill bribe the sexton for your grave.' The ghost then vanished gaily,
Crying, 'Bless you, wicked Captain Smith, remember poor Miss Bailey.'
Oh, Miss Bailey! unfortunate Miss Bailey.

*Miss
Bailey's
Ghost*

Anonymous

Drugged

Walter de la Mare
1873–1961

Inert in his chair,
In a candle's guttering glow;
His bottle empty,
His fire sunk low;
With drug-sealed lids shut fast,
Unsated mouth ajar,
This darkened phantasm walks
Where nightmares are:

In a frenzy of life and light,
Crisscross – a menacing throng –
They jibe, they squeal at the stranger,
Jostling along,
Their faces cadaverous grey:
While on high from an attic stare
Horrors, in beauty apparelled,
Down the dark air.

A stream gurgles over its stones,
The chambers within are a-fire.
Stumble his shadowy feet
Through shine, through mire;
And the flames leap higher.
In vain yelps the wainscot mouse;
In vain beats the hour;
Vacant his body must drowse
Until daybreak flower –

Staining these walls with its rose,
And the draughts of the morning shall stir
Cold on cold brow, cold hands.
And the wanderer
Back to flesh house must return.
Lone soul – in horror to see,
Than dream more meagre and awful,
Reality.

There was a land where lived no violets.
A traveller at once demanded: 'Why?'
The people told him:
'Once the violets of this place spoke thus:
"Until some woman freely gives her lover
To another woman
We will fight in bloody scuffle." '
Sadly the people added:
'There are no violets here.'

*There
Was a
Land*

*Stephen Crane
1871–1900*

I saw a ship of martial build
(Her standards set, her brave apparel on)
Directed as by madness mere
Against a stolid iceberg steer,
Nor budge it, though the infatuate ship went down.
The impact made huge ice-cubes fall
Sullen, in tons that crashed the deck;
But that one avalanche was all —
No other movement save the foundering wreck.

Along the spurs of ridges pale,
Not any slenderest shaft and frail,
A prism over glass-green gorges lone,
Toppled; nor lace of traceries fine,
Nor pendant drops in grot or mine
Were jarred, when the stunned ship went down.
Nor sole the gulls in cloud that wheeled
Circling one snow-flanked peak afar,
But nearer fowl the floes that skimmed
And crystal beaches, felt no jar.

No thrill transmitted stirred the lock
Of jack-straw needle-ice at base;
Towers undermined by waves — the block
Atilt impending — kept their place.
Seals, dozing sleek on sliddery ledges
Slipt never, when by loftier edges
Through very inertia overthrown,
The impetuous ship in bafflement went down.

*The
Berg*

A Dream

*Herman
Melville
1819–91*

157

Hard Berg (methought), so cold, so vast,
With mortal damps self-overcast;
Exhaling still thy dankish breath –
Adrift dissolving, bound for death;
Though lumpish thou, a lumbering one –
A lumbering lubbard loitering slow,
Impingers rue thee and go down,
Sounding thy precipice below,
Nor stir the slimy slug that sprawls
Along thy dead indifference of walls.

Prisoner's Dream

*Shakespeare
(from
'Richard III')
1564–1616*

Methoughts that I had broken from the Tower,
And was embarked to cross to Burgundy,
And in my company was my brother Gloucester,
Who from my cabin tempted me to walk
Upon the hatches. Thence we looked toward England,
And cited up a thousand heavy times,
During the wars of York and Lancaster
That had befall'n us. As we paced along
Upon the giddy footing of the hatches,
Methought that Gloucester stumbled, and in falling
Struck me, that thought to stay him, overboard,
Into the tumbling billows of the main.
O Lord, methought what pain it was to drown!
What sights of ugly death within mine eyes!
Methoughts I saw a thousand fearful wracks;
A thousand men that fishes gnawed upon;
Wedges of gold, great ingots, heaps of pearl,
Inestimable stones, unvalued jewels,
All scatt'red in the bottom of the sea.
Some lay in dead men's skulls; and in the holes
Where eyes did once inhabit there were crept,
As 'twere in scorn of eyes, reflecting gems,
That wooed the slimy bottom of the deep,
And mocked the dead bones that lay scatt'red by.

God came to Abram,
Abram the man
Who knew no glory
Could resist God's ban,
And God said: '*Abram,*
I come to destroy
Sodom, Sodom,
Sodom, Sodom,
That golden city
Of sin and joy.'

Ballad
of the
Trial of
Sodom

Vernon
Watkins
1906–67

Thunder. Thunder. Thunder. Thunder.
Death is terrible, a thing of wonder.
First is a lethargy that no man likes,
Then comes the moment when the lightning strikes.

Then Abram, trying
To save that place,
Thinking of the dying,
Fell upon his face.
'Lord if there were fifty
Righteous men
In Sodom, Sodom,
Sodom, Sodom,
Men who were steadfast,
Would you destroy it then?'

Heaven knows what payment
An advocate should ask,
But old man Abram
Had the hardest task.
He looked at Sodom
And he heard God's voice:
'*Sodom, Sodom,*
Sodom, Sodom;
Hide not the city
That my hand destroys.'

And Abram was trying
To save that place.
He lay for a long time
And could not lift his face.
'*White though the lightning*
Where the thunder rolls

Towards Sodom, Sodom,
Sodom, Sodom,
I shall not destroy it
If there are fifty souls.'

And Abram pondered.
He could not make amends.
It lightened and thundered.
He counted up his friends.
'Lord God, have patience.
May flesh be left alive
In Sodom, Sodom,
Sodom, Sodom,
That doomed city,
If the fifty lack five?'

The Lord God darkened
Like a fiery cloud.
Abram waited
As he lay there bowed;
He saw Hell's demons
In a midnight dive
In Sodom, Sodom,
Sodom, Sodom.
'I shall not destroy it
For the forty-and-five.'

'Lord God, have patience.
Destruction is just;
To hide the accursed
In the darkest dust.
But should there be forty
In the temple found
Of Sodom, Sodom,
Sodom, Sodom,
Then would you brand it,
Raze it to the ground?'

Abram breathed.
A long breath he took.
He thought of the temple,
And the temple shook.
Monsters of sacrilege
Sprawled where it stood

In Sodom, Sodom,
Sodom, Sodom,
'I would not brand it
For the forty good.'

And Abram knew,
Abram knew,
This was the hardest
Peace for which to sue.
'Lord God, forgive me
That I should speak again
Of Sodom, Sodom,
Sodom, Sodom.
Would you spare the city
For thirty good men?'

Thunder. Thunder. Thunder. Thunder.
Death is terrible, a thing of wonder.
First is a lethargy that no man likes,
Then comes the moment when the lightning strikes.

And Abram counted.
Try as he would,
He could not make the number up
To thirty good.
The Judgment's answer
Came upon him then:
'Tell Sodom, Sodom,
Sodom, Sodom,
I shall not destroy it
For thirty good men.'

Abram was silent.
Abram was dumb.
He heard Hell's demons
Beating on a drum.
He saw men carried
Under long, slim poles
Through Sodom, Sodom,
Sodom, Sodom.
'Lord, would you save it
For twenty souls?'

This was the last time.
This was the last.
Now for the brimstone
And the blinding blast.
He saw huge darkness
Like a hangman's hood
On Sodom, Sodom,
Sodom, Sodom.
'I still would spare it
For the twenty good.'

'Lord, thou art just.
Lord, thou art just.
How should we utter
Who are less than dust?
Yet so wicked
Are the hearts of men
In Sodom, Sodom,
Sodom, Sodom.
Still would you spare it
If the good were ten?'

Fearful the silence,
Fearful the span
Stretching that moment
Between God and man.
Abram sweated
His life out then
For Sodom, Sodom,
Sodom, Sodom.
'I shall not destroy it
If the good are ten.'

Abram the father
Counting up the cost
Saw faith plainly
And knew that he had lost.
God looked at Sodom
In that pleading place,
Sodom, Sodom,
Sodom, Sodom.
Down looked Abram,
And he lost his case.

reasury at Petra

Redemp-tion

George Herbert
1593-1633

Having been tenant long to a rich Lord,
  Not thriving, I resolvèd to be bold,
And make a suit unto Him, to afford
  A new small-rented lease, and cancell th'ola.

In heaven at His manour I Him sought:
  They told me there, that He was lately gone
About some land, which he had deerly bought
  Long since on Earth, to take possession.

I straight return'd, and knowing His great birth,
  Sought Him accordingly in great resorts –
  In cities, theatres, gardens, parks, and courts:
At length I heard a raggèd noise and mirth

  Of theeves and murderers; there I Him espied,
  Who straight, 'Your suit is granted,' said, and died.

Ghost Crabs

Ted Hughes
b. 1930

At nightfall, as the sea darkens,
A depth darkness thickens, mustering from the gulfs and the submarine
    badlands,
To the sea's edge. To begin with
It looks like rocks uncovering, mangling their pallor.
Gradually the labouring of the tide
Falls back from its productions,
Its power slips back from glistening nacelles, and they are crabs.
Giant crabs, under flat skulls, staring inland
Like a packed trench of helmets.
Ghosts, they are ghost-crabs.
They emerge
An invisible disgorging of the sea's cold
Over the man who strolls along the sands.
They spill inland, into the smoking purple
Of our woods and towns – a bristling surge
Of tall and staggering spectres
Gliding like shocks through water.
Our walls, our bodies, are no problem to them.
Their hungers are going elsewhere.
We cannot see them or turn our minds from them.

Their bubbling mouths, their eyes
In a slow mineral fury
Press through our nothingness where we sprawl on our beds,
Or sit in our rooms. Our dreams are ruffled maybe.
Or we jerk awake to the world or our possessions
With a gasp, in a sweat burst, brains jamming blind
Into the bulb-light. Sometimes, for minutes, a sliding
Staring
Thickness of silence
Presses between us. These crabs own this world.
All night, around us or through us,
They stalk each other, they fasten on to each other,
They mount each other, they tear each other to pieces,
They utterly exhaust each other.
They are the powers of this world.
We are their bacteria,
Dying their lives and living their deaths.
At dawn, they sidle back under the sea's edge.
They are the turmoil of history, the convulsion
In the roots of blood, in the cycles of concurrence.
To them, our cluttered countries are empty battleground.
All day they recuperate under the sea.
Their singing is like a thin sea-wind flexing in the rocks of a headland,

Where only crabs listen.

They are God's only toys.

O world invisible, we view thee,
O world intangible, we touch thee,
O world unknowable, we know thee,
Inapprehensible, we clutch thee!

Does the fish soar to find the ocean,
The eagle plunge to find the air —
That we ask of the stars in motion
If they have rumour of thee there?

Not where the wheeling systems darken,
And our benumbed conceiving soars! —

The Kingdom
of God

'In no strange land'

*Francis
Thompson
1859–1907*

Sea cave

The drift of pinions, would we hearken,
Beats at our own clay-shuttered doors.

The angels keep their ancient places; —
Turn but a stone, and start a wing!
'Tis ye, 'tis your estrangèd faces,
That miss the many-splendoured thing.

But (when so sad thou canst not sadder)
Cry; — and upon thy so sore loss
Shall shine the traffic of Jacob's ladder
Pitched between Heaven and Charing Cross.

Yea, in the night, my Soul, my daughter,
Cry, — clinging Heaven by the hems;
And lo, Christ walking on the water
Not of Gennesareth, but Thames!

The Labyrinth

Edwin Muir
1887–1959

Since I emerged that day from the labyrinth,
Dazed with the tall and echoing passages,
The swift recoils, so many I almost feared
I'd meet myself returning at some smooth corner,
Myself or my ghost, for all there was unreal
After the straw ceased rustling and the bull
Lay dead upon the straw and I remained,
Blood-splashed, if dead or alive I could not tell
In the twilight nothingness (I might have been
A spirit seeking his body through the roads
Of intricate Hades) — ever since I came out
To the world, the still fields swift with flowers, the trees
All bright with blossom, the little green hills, the sea,
The sky and all in movement under it,
Shepherds and flocks and birds and the young and old,
(I stared in wonder at the young and the old,
For in the maze time had not been with me;

I had strayed, it seemed, past sun and season and change,
Past rest and motion, for I could not tell
At last if I moved or stayed; the maze itself
Revolved around me on its hidden axis
And swept me smoothly to its enemy,
The lovely world) – since I came out that day,
There have been times when I have heard my footsteps
Still echoing in the maze, and all the roads
That run through the noisy world, deceiving streets
That meet and part and meet, and rooms that open
Into each other – and never a final room –
Stairways and corridors and antechambers
That vacantly wait for some great audience,
The smooth sea-tracks that open and close again,
Tracks undiscoverable, indecipherable,
Paths on the earth and tunnels underground,
And bird-tracks in the air – all seemed a part
Of the great labyrinth. And then I'd stumble
In sudden blindness, hasten, almost run,
As if the maze itself were after me
And soon must catch me up. But taking thought,
I'd tell myself, 'You need not hurry. This
Is the good firm earth. All roads lie free before you.'
But my bad spirit would sneer, 'No, do not hurry.
No need to hurry. Haste and delay are equal
In this one world, for there's no exit, none,
No place to come to, and you'll end where you are,
Deep in the centre of the endless maze.'

I could not live if this were not illusion.
It is a world, perhaps; but there's another.
For once in a dream or trance I saw the gods
Each sitting on the top of his mountain-isle,
While down below the little ships sailed by,
Toy multitudes swarmed in the harbours, shepherds drove
Their tiny flocks to the pastures, marriage feasts
Went on below, small birthdays and holidays,
Ploughing and harvesting and life and death,
And all permissible, all acceptable,
Clear and secure as in a limpid dream.
But they, the gods, as large and bright as clouds,
Conversed across the sounds in tranquil voices
High in the sky above the untroubled sea;

And their eternal dialogue was peace
Where all these things were woven; and this our life
Was as a chord deep in that dialogue,
As easy utterance of harmonious words,
Spontaneous syllables bodying forth a world.

That was the real world; I have touched it once,
And now shall know it always. But the lie,
The maze, the wild-wood waste of falsehood, roads
That run and run and never reach an end,
Embowered in error – I'd be prisoned there
But that my soul has birdwings to fly free.

Oh these deceits are strong almost as life.
Last night I dreamt I was in the labyrinth,
And woke far on. I did not know the place.

My Soul, there is a Countrie
        Far beyond the stars,
Where stands a winged Centrie
        All skilfull in the wars,
There above noise, and danger
        Sweet peace sits crown'd with smiles,
And one born in a Manger
        Commands the Beauteous files,
He is thy gracious friend,
        And (O my Soul awake!)
Did in pure love descend
        To die here for thy sake,
If thou canst get but thither,
        There growes the flowre of peace,
The Rose that cannot wither,
        Thy fortresse, and thy ease;
Leave then thy foolish ranges;
        For none can thee secure,
But one, who never changes,
        Thy God, thy life, thy Cure.

Peace

Henry
Vaughan
1622–95

Up-Helly-Aa Festival

What would I do forever in a big place, who
have lived all my life in a small island?
The same parish holds the cottage I was born in, all
my family, and the cool churchyard.
                              I have looked
up at the stars from my front verandah and have been afraid
of their pathless distances. I have never flown
in the loud aircraft nor have I seen palaces,
so I would prefer not to be taken up high nor
rewarded with a large mansion.
                              I would like
to remain half-drowsing through an evening light
watching bamboo trees sway and ruffle for a valley-wind,
to remember old times but not to live them again;
occasionally to have a good meal with no milk
nor honey for I don't like them, and now and then to walk
by the grey sea-beach with two old dogs and watch
men bring up their boats from the water.
                              For all this,
for my hope of heaven, I am willing to forgive my debtors
and to love my neighbour . . .
                              although the wretch throws stones
at my white rooster and makes too much noise in her damn backyard.

An Old Jamaican Woman Thinks About the Hereafter

A. L. Hendriks
b. 1922

*

At the round earths imagin'd corners, blow
Your trumpets, Angells, and arise, arise
From death, you numberlesse infinities
Of soules, and to your scattered bodies goe,
All whom the flood did, and fire shall o'erthrow,
All whom warre, dearth, age, agues, tyrannies,
Despaire, law, chance hath slaine, and you whose eyes,
Shall behold God, and never tast deaths woe.
But let them sleepe, Lord, and mee mourne a space,
For, if above all these, my sinnes abound,
'Tis late to aske abundance of thy grace,
When wee are there; here on this lowly ground,
Teach me how to repent; for that's as good
As if thou'hadst seal'd my pardon, with thy blood.

Sonnet

John Donne
1572–1631

Christmas

A. L. Hendriks
b. 1922

Never before and never again
has the blue air of Earth opened
to receive so accurate a shape,
nor the apparent world of heights
and deeps and thicknesses gaped
and altered its proportions for such a form.

On that morning there was a shattering
of conventional concepts, shadows
seemed to curve longer, habitual planes
and surfaces flowed into new angles, moulds
we knew and trusted appeared wider,
and all the colours,
line
and patterns
we were accustomed to, uttered a cry
of freedom and plunged out
to a greater sky.
                    Walls
that had been made hard, stirred
with a slow movement, stones
that previously lay inert, flexed
and turned; and the stiff wood
of beams and cross-trees stretched
and quivered to the keener sight.

What then of water, seas and lakes?
How they became awake, (lively as fish
themselves,) swimming and flashing;
breaking over new shores; and mirroring
trees, animals and birds
that leaned above them, more vital than they!

But it was in people,
in Earth-surrounded people,
that the marvel was strongest: men
who were anxious for their breathing,
and all requirements of the flesh, (bread,
cattle, silver,) and troubled by its limits,
suddenly,
            (for in this matter years
and centuries are brief, brief periods,)

suddenly
       flung down their images,
loosened their hold of the possessive soil
and claimed no horizon.

Over to You

The mind's eye often sees with peculiar vividness, while dreams may seem more important than reality. In DREAMS AND VISIONS the poet's imagination conveys a special kind of truth.

The Chimney Sweep   (i) Tom's dream comforts him as he and the other boys begin work. Describe the beginning of the day's work and how the various boys tackle it. (ii) Perhaps by the end of the day Tom is miserable and has a sombre dream that night. Describe the dream and the moment of awaking.

The Little Black Boy and *The Chimney Sweep*   Blake was a painter as well as a poet and these poems may suggest pictures to you. Try to see some of Blake's pictures and suggest how he might have illustrated either or both of these poems.

After Apple-Picking   (i) Imagine you are the speaker and tell of a few moments not recorded by the poet as the apple-picking draws to a close. Suggest something of the picker's dazed state as tiredness comes over him. (ii) What kind of things perhaps 'troubled' the sleep of the picker?

Dese Bones Gwine To Rise Again   Once again, if you can sing this ballad, so much the better. If not, you could have several people chanting the chorus (which can come as the second and fourth line of each verse) while the narrator tells the story. An accompaniment of humming on a small range of notes could also be effective.

I Know Some Lonely Houses   Do you think the robbery took place?

Miss Bailey's Ghost   Here you need a narrator, a chorus, Captain Smith and Miss Bailey, who needs a ghostly voice which fades into the distance. (i) Recount the meeting between Miss Bailey and the Sexton as she offers the bribe.

Drugged   (i) At midday the addict resolves to do without his drug for once, but by evening he has given in again. What thoughts and actions fill the interval? (ii) Give the addict's impression of the 'awful reality' around him as he returns to consciousness.

The Berg   Keeping the dream atmosphere, describe more fully (i) the approach of the ship to the iceberg, (ii) the ship sinking through the water.

Prisoner's Dream   Imagine that the dream continues. Some of the drowned men appear to come to life, though they do not speak. The dreamer tries to escape but cannot. Describe the scene and the action.

Ballad of the Trial of Sodom   (i) Give your ideas on how this poem could be dramatised without further dialogue. Consider the use of tape-recorded voices, painted backgrounds, choruses, mime, etc. (ii) Choose another Old Testament story (for example, Noah, Job, Isaac, Jonah) and write a piece in similar style. Another look at the Genesis story in *Dese Bones Gwine To Rise Again* might prove helpful.

Drugged; Prisoner's Dream; Ghost Crabs (i) These poems present horrific images. Which of the three seems to you most compelling? Why? (ii) Describe a nightmare with sea, caves, land, forest, a city, or several of these as setting.

An Old Jamaican Woman Thinks About the Hereafter (i) Imagine the old woman chatting to a friend about the day's events. What has she to say? (ii) Suppose that her son, who considers himself more up to date than his mother, gives *his* picture of 'the hereafter'. Write what he says.

Christmas You might like to read this poem in conjunction with *Ballad of the Bread Man* (Section I), *Christmas at Sea* (Section III) and *little tree* (Section VI) as a small Christmas anthology. The Christmas poems mentioned in the reading list and the sermon in Eliot's *Murder in the Cathedral* might make useful additions. Some parts of the Nativity story in St Matthew 1 and 2 could provide linking passages, and if you were making a tape-recording you could include snatches of Christmas carols, children telling what presents they wanted, the snap of crackers, etc. But remember that some skilful editing will be needed!

– *The section as a whole*

(i) The first four poems deal with childhood. What facets of childhood not included in these would make good subjects for imaginative poems? Suggest the sort of scene, incident, dream or 'vision' that might make a suitable starting point in each case.

(ii) Perhaps the most difficult poem here is *The Labyrinth,* in which the poet uses a very old story to symbolise his feelings about life. You might be able to use other legends (for example, that of Icarus, who tried to fly too near the sun, or Midas, whose touch turned everything to gold) in a modern setting to illustrate some basic truth.

(iii) Some of the poems give us impressions of heaven, but writers offer fewer visions of hell than formerly. Why is this? What terrors might a modern version of hell contain?

(iv) Re-read *The Berg,* perhaps in conjunction with *The Convergence of the Twain* (Section III), and write an imaginative piece about a cave or glacier or dead volcano.

(v) Which two poems might be illustrated by (i) an imaginative film, (ii) a surrealist painting? (It might help you here to look at some of the paintings of Dali or Magritte.)

(vi) Which of the dreams and visions seem to suggest escape? What is the dreamer escaping from? Do you sympathise?

Further Reading *

If you enjoyed the poems where scenes are evoked in great detail, you would find 'Poem in October' (D. Thomas: 10) and 'Tarantella' (Belloc: 2) in some respects similar. 'Moonlit Apples' (Drinkwater: 1) and 'The Lotos-Eaters' (Tennyson: 7) take us further into the realms of the imagination. Evocations of past people and events are in Dickinson's 'The Roman Wall' (11); Kirkup's 'To the Ancestral North' (11); R. S. Thomas's 'Welsh History' (11); MacNeice's 'Wessex Guidebook' (7); Eliot's 'Journey of the Magi' (2, 12); Keats' 'The Eve of Saint Agnes' (7); Housman's 'On Wenlock Edge' (4) and Stevenson's 'Armies in the Fire' (1). Some further poems on Christmas are MacNeice's 'Christmas Shopping' (12) and Betjeman's 'Christmas' (10, 11). Poems depending on different types of fantasy are 'The History of the Flood' (Heath-Stubbs: 6, 9); R. Lowell's 'Mr Edwards and the Spider' (13); Graves' 'Lollocks' (7); Blake's 'And Did Those Feet' (2); Coleridge's 'Kubla Khan' (2), 'The Ancient Mariner' and 'Christabel' (Os); 'The Demon Lover' (2); 'Jabberwocky' (L. Carroll) and 'The Dong with the Luminous Nose' (Lear) in 2; Rossetti's 'The Blessed Damozel' (4); Graves' 'Welsh Incident' (12) and Arnold's 'The Forsaken Merman' (1). Of a more visionary or symbolic nature are 'Sailing to Byzantium' (Yeats: 8, 10); 'And Death shall Have No Dominion' (D. Thomas: 4, 10); 'I Think Continually' (Spender: 4); 'Ode on a Grecian Urn' (Keats: 4); 'if there are any heavens' (Cummings: *Selected Poems:* F) and – perhaps in extracts – 'The Waste Land' (Eliot: *Selected Poems:* F).

Some prose works of the past remain as compelling as ever in the field of fantasy, for example, Christian's meeting with Apollyon and Passing the Valley of the Shadow in *Pilgrim's Progress* (P); Swift's *Gulliver's Travels,* e.g. Bk. II: Brobdingnag (P); Mary Shelley's *Frankenstein* (D); *The Tales of Hoffmann* (B); De Quincey's *Confessions of an English Opium Eater* (last section) (D); L. Carroll's *Alice in Wonderland* and *Through the Looking Glass* (N); Wilde's *Picture of Dorian Gray* (P) and Poe's *Tales of Mystery and Imagination* (D). Modern short stories dealing with memory or imagination are 'The Peaches' (D. Thomas: 18); 'The Secret Life of Walter Mitty' (Thurber: 18); 'The Man in the Moon' (Ustinov in *English Short Stories of Today,* 3rd Series: O); 'Rats' (Haldane: 16); 'The Portobello Road' and 'The Seraph and the Zambesi' in *The Go-Away Bird* by M. Spark (P). Such tales of mystery as *King Solomon's Mines* (R. Haggard: L) and *The Hound of the Baskervilles* (Conan Doyle: MU) still retain their force but must now compete with the vast realm of science fiction. Wells remains the key name here, in such works as *The Time Machine* (H), *The War of the Worlds* (H), *The First Men in the Moon* (H) and *The Man Who Could Work Miracles* (16). John Wyndham with *The Chryalids, The Day of the Triffids* (P) and a half a dozen others claims many young readers. Writers distinguished in other fields have also contributed, e.g.

* For explanation of symbols see p. 30.

C. S. Lewis: *Out of the Silent Planet* (L); E. M. Forster: 'The Machine Stops' (in *Collected Short Stories :* (P); Fred Hoyle: *The Black Cloud* and (with G. Hoyle) *Fifth Planet* (P); and A. Huxley: *Brave New World* (CW). The following are interesting collections: *The Best from Fantasy and S.F.* (Ferman: G); *The Starlit Corridor* (Mansfield: PER); *Aspects of Science Fiction* (Docherty: MU). The world of legend is, however, by no means dead, as witnessed by the great popularity of Tolkien's *The Hobbit* (L) and *The Lord of The Rings* (AU), the last section of which, describing the entry to Mordor, competes with much science fiction. The older myths may be read in Graves' *Greek Myths and Legends* (CAS) and *Norse Legends and Myths* (Ed. Walsh: L).

Bridie's *Tobias and the Angel* (CON) recreates an old story in dramatic form. *The Long Sunset* (L) by R. C. Sherriff is based on the King Arthur story, while Willis Hall's *The Gentle Knight* (B) is a satirical fairy-tale. Many nativity plays seek a fresh approach to the Christmas story, e.g. *Four Nativity Plays* by J. Hadden (L). *A Journey to the Centre of the Earth* is dramatised in *May We Recommend, Bk 2, 2nd series* (L). The supernatural element in the Elizabethan theatre (e.g. *Dr Faustus* (Marlowe: O), *Hamlet, Macbeth* and *The Tempest* (Shakespeare: O)) might offer you a rewarding field of study. A modern play which creates a composite vision of a small town is *Under Milk Wood* by D. Thomas (D), while realism and symbol merge in *Waiting for Godot* (Beckett: F).